DEDICATION

These words do not belong to the author anymore than they belong to the people quoted in the book: Norbert Wiener, Karl Lashley, George Kubler, J. Z. Young, John Lilly, Marshall McLuhan, Stuart Brand, Heinz von Foerster, Edward T. Hall, Alfred North Whitehead, W. Grey Walter, Kenneth Sayre, René Descartes, Benjamin Lee Whorf, Niels Bohr, René Dubos, D. and K. Stanley-Jones, John Lucas, Carlos Castenedas, Sören Kierkegaard, Wilder Penfield, R. G. Bickford, Edmund Carpenter, Werner Heisenberg, Sir James Jeans, Ludwig Wittgenstein, Wallace Stevens, Leon Brillouin, T. S. Eliot, I. A. Richards, Gertrude Stein, Max Born, J. Andrade e Silva, P. W. Bridgman, R. Buckminster Fuller, Sir Arthur Eddington, William Empson, C. G. Jung, Bertrand Russell, William Butler Yeats, John McHale, Rudolph Wurlitzer, Ihab Hassan, T. E. Hulme, Simone Weil, Samuel Beckett, David Pears, Alain Robbe-Grillet, Victor Gioscia, Hugo von Hofmannsthal, Norman O. Brown, William Shakespeare, E. E. Cummings, Paul Valery, Ezra Pound, Henry Miller.

These words belong to the reader.

John Brockman

BOOKS BY JOHN BROCKMAN

As Author:

BY THE LATE JOHN BROCKMAN

37

As Editor:

REAL TIME

AFTERWORDS

By John Brockman

Anchor Books
Anchor Press / Doubleday
Garden City, New York
1973

Anchor Books Edition: 1973
Part I of this book is revised from *By the Late John Brockman*, The Macmillan Company, 1969.
Part II of this book is revised from *37*, by John Brockman, Holt, Rinehart and Winston, 1970.
ISBN: 0-385-01554-2
Library of Congress Catalog Card Number 72–92254

Printed in the United States of America

ACKNOWLEDGMENTS: Please refer to the end of this book for the source of many quotations throughout the text.

I

Man is dead.

The choice is between the present and the past. The choice is between choice and no choice. There is no choice.

Man is dead, and all the categories that created and characterized human existence must be reconsidered. The key to elimination of words? Ownership. Replace all words pertaining to ownership with words concerning functions, operations. What did man own? Consciousness, feelings, emotions, mind, ego, spirit, soul, pain, etc., words resulting from centuries of belief, and no longer useful.

Consciousness does not exist; indeed, there is no reason to believe that it ever did exist. Not conscious, not unconscious. If consciousness does not exist, there can hardly be a state of unconsciousness.

Man is an abstraction. Human abstractions are based on the past, on behavior, not on operant considerations of what is happening. Considerations of the present? Patterns. Transaction. Activity. Doing. Considerations of the past? Behavior. Environment. Man.

The abstractions of man characterize phenomena without regard to the operant activities of the phenomena. It is a limited system of classification.

How to deal with what is happening? Search for rhythms and patterns. Man is dead. The analysis moves from the study of fixed entities that are capable of ownership to the transaction of the species with environmental forces. Look to the transaction. The world about us is accessible only through a nervous system, and our information concerning it is confined to what limited information the nervous system can transmit. The brain receives information and acts on it by telling the effectors what to do. The loop is completed as the performance of the effectors provides new information for the brain. It is a new feedback loop, a nonlinear relationship between output and input.

Man always dealt with what had already happened, believing that it occurred in the present instant. What he thought was happening coincides approximately between steps two and three of the loop. Man was aware only of the past, and never aware of the activities of his brain, where there are order and arrangement, but there is no experience of the creation of that order. Experience gives us no clue as to the means by which it is organized. If the organization were produced by a slide rule or a digital computer, consciousness would give no indication of that fact nor any basis for denying it. If the brain is capable of producing such organization, then it may be considered the organizer.

To understand these notions, it is necessary to explore the concept of the interval. The interval refers to the moment of the creation of the order of the brain's activity. The activity of which man was never aware, the inaccessible present, the direct experience of the brain. The rest of time emerges only in signals relayed to us at this instant by innumerable stages and unexpected bearers. The nature of a signal is that its message is neither here nor now, but there and then. If it is a signal, it is a past action, no longer embraced by the "now" of present being. The perception of a signal happens "now," but its impulse happened then. In any event, the present instant is the plane upon which the signals of all being are projected. This instant, the interval, constitutes all that is directly experienced. It was for man the abstraction, his Achilles' heel.

In this evolutionary stage, a stage beyond space and time, the interval is closed forever, and man ceases to exist.

Man ordered his experience in terms of psychological considerations of the nonexistent mind. But the ordering of experience is always on the here-and-now level. The interpretation of the ordering is always at the there-and-then level. Be aware that the brain's operation is a continuing activity of ordering in the here-and-now. There was always ordering in the here-and-now while man deluded himself with considerations there-and-then, considerations of a world that didn't exist. A world that never had existed. The world of the past. A fractional instant, and yet the past. Because of that interval man was able to exist. Man, a relic of the instantaneous past. Man, an instant too old to exist. Things not existent should be of no interest to us. All those things rendered unto man are based on a system that deals with illusion. The interpretation of the ordering of the brain takes place while new ordering is continually happening. It is almost as though there were two parallel planes.

Almost. We might even assume there was a choice between living in one plane or another. Actually, there is no choice. There is no choice. There is only the ordering and arrangement, the here-and-now. Some of us, most of us, cannot recognize this level and continue by blindness, by inertia, by pretension, the delusion that we are men. It's a mistake. Man is dead. Man never existed at all. Our awareness as experience is past experience. Dreaming.

Man is dead. It's a world of information. Information in this context refers to regulation and control and has nothing to do with meaning, ideas, or data. Any system is said to be able to receive information if when a change occurs the system is capable of reactions in such a way as to maintain its own stability. Information is nothing but an abstraction. As an abstraction it will allow for new observations and associations, for discernment of patterns and organization. Note that the reference is to a reaction to change. The concern here is only with the reaction, the effect. Information is a measure of the effect. This refers to how the control center of the organism, the brain, reacts to change in order to maintain continuity.

We are dealing with activity integrated on the neural, the brain level, *i.e.*, the present. Thus, when discussing information, we are talking about the brain's response in terms of present, direct experience. This response is always effected without consent or awareness. There is no choice. There is no information unless there is a change. Information does not exist as information until it is within the higher levels of abstraction of each of the minds and computed as such. Up to the point at which it becomes perceived as information, it is signals. These signals travel through the external reality between the two bodies, and travel as signals within the brain substances themselves. Till the complex patterns of traveling neuronal impulses in the brain are computed as information within the cerebral cortex, they are not yet information. Information is the result of a long series of computations based on data signal inputs, data signal transmissions to the brain substance, and recomputations of these data. Information is an abstraction to be used for measuring the communication of pattern, order, and neural inhibition.

What is the information from an electric light bulb? No information. What is the information from a book? No information. To speak of a change as giving information implies that there is somewhere a receiver able to react appropriately to the change. Be concerned only with the changes in the operations of the receiver, the brain, in terms of the transactional present. Do not confuse information with signals or the source of signals. The mind of the observer-participant is where the information is constructed, by and through his own programs, his own rules of perception, his own cognitive and logical processes, his own metaprogram of priorities among programs. His own vast internal computer constructs information from signals and stored bits of signals. Information is a process. There are no sources of information; there are no linear movements of information to the brain.

Information is an abstraction. Information is a measure of effect. Information is a concept that allows for relationships not previously possible. Effect deals with the construction of information from both incoming signals and bits of signals stored in the operant circuits of the brain. The incoming signals are transmitted by both internal and external receptors. Effect involves the total situation and not a single level of information movement. There are no single levels of information movement. The total situation is the neural situation, the process of the nervous system. This system is operational. All that's traceably happening is a shimmering array of pattern shifting occurring in a centerless, edgeless network. It's measurable piecemeal: trivial. The whole is unmeasurable indeed except through effects. Information is the measure of effect, the measure of the ordering of the brain's activity in the transactional present.

Communications theory is the study of messages. In this system, the message is nonlinear. The communication, the message, is pattern, order, neural inhibition. The message is the change in neural activity. It can be considered as a program, and a program is nothing else but a set of commands: "do this; do that . . ." which in other words means: "don't do this; don't do that. . . ." We are dealing with the transmission of neural pattern from a brain and its outputs, through a specifiable set of processes to the external world, through a portion of that world with specifiable modes, media and artificial means to another body, another brain. We are dealing with a set of relationships which allows us to conceptualize the communication of neural experience. The difference between human experience and neural experience is the difference between illusion and reality, between choice and no choice.

In talking about the state of consciousness, do not deal in there-and-then considerations of interpretation of the ordering and arrangement of the direct experience of the brain. The ordering and arrangement are a continual functional happening. The ordering and arrangement are all that is actually happening. Nothing else ever happens. The ordering and arrangement are to be measured in terms of information.

The most significant, the most critical, inventions of man were not those ever considered to be inventions but those which appeared to be innate and natural. Man never understood to what degree all of nature was man-made. One such major and crucial invention was talking. Talking was probably man's most important invention. It was, undoubtedly, considered to be innate and natural until a man, making a new observation, exclaimed, "We're talking." At that point no one had ever heard of such a thing. Still, talking was an invention that changed the way the brain worked. Talking, a man-made invention, provided information modifying the operation of the brain without any awareness. There was no choice. For thousands of years man was molding himself in a certain manner, but the pattern was not invented until a man said, "We're talking."

Man is dead. Credit his death to an invention. The invention was the grasping of a conceptual whole, a set of relationships which had not been previously recognized. The invention was man-made. It was the recognition that reality was communicable. The process was the transmission of neural pattern. Such patterns are electrical, not mental. The system of communication and control functioned without individual human awareness or consent. The message in the system was not words, ideas, images, etc. The message was nonlinear: operant neural pattern. It became clear that new concepts of communication and control involved a new interpretation of man, of man's knowledge of the universe, and of society. Man is dead. "We're talking."

The system can be comprehended only by killing off man. We are not destroying a phenomenon. We are replacing one system of abstraction with another system of abstraction. Man was nothing but a model, a technique. It is now necessary to construct a new model, to invoke a new system of abstraction, no more truthful than the old one, no closer to any ultimate answer. An abstraction is only an abstraction. The insanity of man was that he believed in his humanity as the very basis of reality, as the ultimate end to evolution. But it is of the utmost importance to be vigilant in critically revising modes of abstraction. It is here that philosophy finds its niche as essential to the healthy progress of society. It is the critic of abstractions. A civilization which cannot burst through its current abstractions is doomed to sterility after a very limited period of progress. Man is dead.

This is the end of the doctrine of specific causation. There are only the simultaneous neural operations of the present, the all-at-once, the here-and-now. No more talk about the environment. The only total situation is in what the brain is doing. There is no past, there is no future, there is no time, there is no space. The beginnings, the endings, are all bound up in the multiplicity of neural operations. The unity is methodological. Break through the limited framework of subjects and objects. It's all happening at once, bound up in a universe of simultaneity.

Who's crazy? Mankind went out of its mind. There is no mind out of which to go. Who's crazy?

The supreme abstraction of the brain was indeed the mind. . . . From the confusion of metaphysics and psychoanalysis, abstractions of abstractions, the thinking brain has turned to the first possible glimpses of itself. For years man understood that animals did not act through a consciousness; now it is evident that man himself, the human animal, did not act with a conscious sensibility. It's all a question of breaking through to new systems of abstraction.

Neither the presence nor absence of consciousness can serve as an exclusive criterion either for the presence or absence of any other characteristic in a particular thing. . . . The only way a particular individual can be determined to be conscious is with reference to his observable behavior. Behavior is a consideration of the past. The present is in the activity of the brain. Analyzing the patterns of the present turned the world of man inside out and upside down. Insanity. Who's crazy?

Cogito ergo sum. I think therefore I am. But the only conclusion to be derived from thought is that the brain has direct experience. We are not concerned with the existence of thought but with the activity of the brain.

There is no conscious self, there is no subconscious, there is no mind. Indeed, the word *mental* is an unfortunate word, a word whose function in our culture is often only to stand in lieu of an intelligent explanation, and which connotes rather a foggy limbo than a cosmic structural order characterized by patterning. Be concerned with discerning operant patterns on the neural level. All experience can be accounted for in terms of neural operations. Only by renouncing an explanation of life in the ordinary sense do we gain a possibility of taking into account its characteristics.

This system of abstraction, based as it is on operant considerations, goes beyond linear systems. Nonlinear processes are composed of interacting elements. Common Western language lends itself to pictorial interpretations. But, the description of many aspects of human existence demands a terminology which is not immediately founded on simple physical pictures. Nonlinear processes can be represented by operant mathematical symbols. Common language is a poor substitute. Pure mathematical symbolism allows us to represent relations for which ordinary verbal expression is imprecise or cumbersome. In this connection, it may be stressed that, just by avoiding the reference to the conscious subject which infiltrates daily language, the use of mathematical symbols secures the unambiguity of definition required for objective description.

A measure of the sum of the parts is larger than the sum of the measure of the parts.

$$F(a+b)>F(a)+F(b)$$
F=measure function of squaring
$$F(a+b)=(a+b)^2=a^2+b^2+2ab$$
and
$$F(a)=a^2,\ F(b)=b^2$$
therefore
$$a^2+b^2+2ab>a^2+b^2$$

The product $2ab$ is nothing else but the measure of the interaction of the two parts a and b, namely the interaction of a with b and b with a. To consider this interaction, start with effect and work backward.

The operation of the brain is a nonlinear process. It is a system of self-organization where given sets of oscillations pull themselves together into a particular frequency band.

Man is dead. We are now concerned with the concept of process. In return for the renunciation of accustomed demands on explanation, it offers a logical means of comprehending wider fields of experience, necessitating proper attention to the placing of object-subject separation. Instead of "man" and "not man," move the object-subject separation one step back to objectify a universe of simultaneous operations: the process of interaction of "man" and "not man," integrated on the level of the neural activity of "man." In this system there is not only a universe, but there are also elements capable of observing this universe. The observation is through a nervous system similar to that of the observer-participant in the universe under consideration. Reality is no longer to be found hidden in the subjects and objects of "man" and "not man."

For discussing integration at the neural level we must look to the interval. The only way to capture that moment is with the death of man, the death of the concept of the individual. It has been demonstrated that the brain responds to change in terms of the information it has already received. The past experience of the person determines the manner of his response to a given stimulus. The primary direct effects of stimuli commonly have little bearing on their ultimate expressions. The brain continually functions during the moment man termed the interval, this functioning being dependent on its physiological construction and stored information. There is no interval. There is only what the brain is doing.

Media do not exist. Media must be considered as a single level of information movement, which is a consideration of the world of the past. There are no linear movements of information. Information is a process. Its whole is measurable only by effect. Be concerned with process, with transaction, not with media. Media are in the world of the past. They are the received signals from there-and-then. The medium is not the message. The medium is the confusion. The message is operational. It is a process.

Information is a process. Not words or ideas, or "I like it," "I don't like it," but the total effect of experience, of the brain's operation. Not ideas or opinions, but the changes brought about by the experience, the neural involvement. Information is a nonlinear relationship established between output and input, the simultaneous universe of experiential feedback of information. Points of view are beside the point.

If media do not exist, neither do separations such as form and content, concepts which belong to the treatment of signals there-and-then. In the simultaneous operations of the brain there is neither form nor content. There is information that directs the brain's activity. All imagined considerations of form and content are considerations of the interpretation of the ordering of direct experience. This is in the past. Be concerned only with the ordering, with the present.

No more talk about media, no more talk of the senses, of perception, etc. Such considerations are presented within a conceptual framework that does not allow us to account for contemporary experience. Be concerned with activity integrated on the neural level. It is a process. The only unit of currency in the process is the neural impulse or permeability-wave. In studying the transmission pattern of these waves we learn that each local area of the cortex interprets the message according to its local pattern of response. Nothing in the message itself can indicate its source of origin. On the integrative neural level there are no visual images, no sounds, no taste, no physical feeling, no odor. It matters nothing whether these trains of neural impulse arise in the ear, the eye, or any other sense organ; they are all the same, they have no more individuality than the elemental dots and dashes of the telegraph code. There is no more of a sound or sight or pain in a nerve impulse during transmission than there is love or grief in the underground lines of the telegraph.

The qualities of a neural impulse bear no relation to the sensory stimulus which sends them on their way. Only the quantity or frequency varies. Forget about signal source; forget about sensory source. The eyes see nothing; the ears hear nothing. Our sensory receptors are capable of transmitting neural impulses that are variable only in two ways—namely, the diameter of the conducting fiber and the strength of the sensory stimulus. The former determines the speed of travel; the latter, the frequency, or distance between members of the procession. The eyes see nothing; the ears hear nothing. Give credit to the brain, where there are no pictures, no sounds. There are only electrical neural impulses. It is these purely physical phenomena, whose qualities are fully prescribed by certain numerical data and determined by the semipermanent structures of the anatomy, which constitute the unit of currency in the nervous system. There is no other form of activity of nerve, no other physical movement in the tissues of the brain, out of which the processes of thought may be constructed.

The brain is the organizer. Seeing, hearing, perception—all take place in the brain. The brain, which sees nothing, hears nothing, knows nothing. Each of the sensory receptors has a reception area in the cortex where neural impulses are received and acted upon in terms of a local pattern of response. If an operation could be devised to change the pathway of the optic nerves so that they delivered their messages to the auditory reception areas of the cortex, and to divert the auditory nerves to the visual area, the patient would hear noises when the lights were turned up, and see patterns and colors when the bell was rung.

The mechanism whereby a sensory receptor which has important information to convey can transmit this information to the cortex of the brain, along a neural axone which is as featureless as a telegraph wire, has interesting properties of a quantitative nature. Two methods are available whereby the stark yes-or-no, which is all that the nerve can carry, may be elaborated into the wealth of sensory detail which actually reaches the brain. One method is to vary the number of nerve fibers engaged in the work of transmission: twenty fibers will convey a message more efficiently than ten fibers. The other method is by modulation of the frequency of the impulses as they follow each other along the single track. It becomes a question of frequencies, or numbers.

Man created a dehumanized, computerized world, a world in which he was nothing more than a number. But it was really the other way around: numbers representing neural patterns had somehow become humanized. From an unambiguous and objective representation of patterns of activity, the number became transformed into "man" and "not man." This arbitrary object-subject separation assured ambiguity, vagueness, and illusion.

How does the picture get put together? It doesn't. All that is happening are volleys of neural impulses. What is the point of attempting to correlate patterns of neural activity to mind, feelings, emotions, etc.? Dispense with these abstractions. They are from another epoch. They are of little usefulness in dealing with operant phenomena.

The basis of living systems is self-organization. The brain organizes its activity in a continuous fashion, always in the present. It incarnates the operations it has performed as operant circuits. It exists and can be talked about only in operant terms on what it does. What it does depends on information it constantly receives informing it about changes in itself, environmental forces, the physiological functions of the body. It uses this information to adapt, to change, to maintain its stability and continuity. Information is not to be confused with the source of information. It is not power. It is an abstraction. It is not energy. It is an invention.

A mathematical theorem holds that for any formal system capable of producing arithmetic there is a truism proving the system which cannot be proven within the system. For man there was consciousness, the system for which there was a truism proving the system which could not be shown to be true within the system. All man was sure of was that he was conscious. End of discussion. He could never tell whether this consciousness was the result of a digital computer, religious incantation, etc.

Information is a measure of effect. Start with effect and work backward. Information is a measure of the operant response the brain makes in terms of its nonlinear experience. Information relates to direct neural coding, to brain imprinting. Understanding the nature of nonlinear communication through the process of information closes the gap, gets rid of the interval. Every instant becomes the ordering of the brain in the simultaneous, continuous present. Even the notion of instants, of time, disappears.

The evolutionary significance of all this is unbelievable, for man. It is the end of importance. It is the end of man.

This exercise merely presents a system, a methodology. No truths are to be found here. The author doesn't believe a word of what is set forth and is not interested in formulation of new dogma. It is the formulation of a system, an abstraction from reality not to be confused with reality. Reality as a whole is unmeasurable except through effect. The unity is in the methodology, in the writing, reading, in the navigation. This system cannot provide us with ultimate answers, nor does it present the ultimate questions. There are none.

The static, fixed, linear system is now superseded by one that is operational and nonlinear. It is important to observe that if the frequency of an oscillator can be changed by impulses of a different frequency, the mechanism must be nonlinear. A linear mechanism acting on an oscillation of a given frequency can produce only oscillation of the same frequency, generally with some change in phase and amplitude. This is not true for nonlinear mechanisms, which may produce oscillations of frequencies which are the sum and differences of different orders, of the frequency of the oscillator and the frequency of the imposed disturbance. There is no information in a linear system. The only way to consider such a system is in terms of the nonexistent past.

Don't look for beginnings, for endings. Navigate through reality with no pretense of knowledge. The unity is methodological. The unity is in the activity and will not lead to any final answer. It is a path. All paths are the same: they lead nowhere. Keep moving.

Man was oblivious to the changes taking place as a result of man-made actions. Had that level been appreciated, television sets might have been viewed in a different light. Within the linear construct he could not see the information patterns. Deaths were caused by fits induced by the flicker of faulty television tubes. Scientific institutes warned that sitting within four feet of color television sets could cause cancer. Yet the same old questions were asked: "Did you like the program?" All the while the information of the television experience was coding the operation of the brain.

Consider that the experience of television violates innate biological rhythms programmed into the genetic homeostatic constitution from the earliest evolutionary eras. These biological rhythms are invisible, yet nevertheless are information in terms of the experience of the brain. The most obvious and perhaps least recognized rhythm is the day/night, light/dark flicker. The experience is a constant input of information for the brain, effecting change without consent or awareness. Note also recent experiments indicating that in all animal species gonadal activity is increased by light rays reaching the retina. . . . As is the case for other biological cycles, interference with the natural cycles of light exposure can result in physiological disturbances. . . . Until the last century, man lived in the dark for long hours during the winter months, and this is still true in many primitive societies. Modern man, in contrast, was exposed to bright light for sixteen hours a day throughout the year. In view of the fact that light rays can affect hormonal activities, and that many, if not most physiological functions are linked to circadian and seasonal cycles, it seems possible that this change in the ways of life had long-range consequences for the human species.

Television, as direct experience, can be considered in this instance on two levels. First, it is a potent source of light. The cathode-ray experience is the only instance where man looked directly into a light source for any sustained period, possibly averaging four hours a day. Light is actually projected onto the retina by the cathode-ray tube. Second, man responded not only to light perceived by the senses but also to factors of biological rhythms such as the day/night flicker. Television alters this rhythm violently. Man talked about the violence evident on television programs. In light of the above considerations he might have developed a "Theory of Neural Programs, Television, and Violence," which hypothesized that "due to circumstances beyond our control, this 'program' is out of order," which is to say that there may well be limits beyond which the natural rhythms are not amenable to frequency-synchronization with new environmental periodicities. Violence.

"We're talking." The direct experience of the brain is communicated. Communicated through information. Man ceased to exist when nonlinear extension of experience was comprehended. It always existed, but now, once again, it's time to say, "We're talking." Thought control? Absolutely. There is one hundred per cent thought control. Indeed, any considerations on this level are beyond man's morality. It is a question of a major leap in evolution.

We are beyond space and time; we are beyond good and evil. There is only information. It is the control, the measure by which the operation of the brain changes. There is always complete control.

Man was always blind to considerations of the present. In the transactional present, man's brain was continually coded through information. This information was of man's own devising. Man determined what he would be, what he would think. This ordering took place in the present. But man, who made the mistake of confusing abstraction and reality, deluded himself into thinking he was conscious, and then proclaimed that this consciousness, this delusion, was reality. There are several stumbling blocks to communication between linear and nonlinear systems. The major one is that linear systems do not exist. All that exists are the operations of the brain, the direct experience, a nonlinear oscillation.

Instead of looking to the world of man, to the linear abstractions, to the conscious motivations, etc., attention must be turned to a universe of control patterns, patterns of complete control, the nonlinear process of neural activity. The message in this system is the communication of pattern. A message need not be the result of a conscious human effort for the transmission of ideas. Work on the level of deciphering the patterns that have always existed but that man hardly even suspected. Consider the notion of power engineering: The main function of power engineering is transmission of energy or power from one place to another with its generation by appropriate generators and its employment by appropriate motors or lamps or other such apparatus. So long as this is not associated with transmission of a particular pattern, as for example in processes of automatic control, power engineering remains a separate entity with its own technique. Man was a separate entity with its own technique. The unity is methodological. Concentrate on communication of operant pattern. The only experience that is real is in the operations of the brain. The individual experience, the private experience, the personal experience: illusion. The end of the individual.

Man concerned himself with meaning. His books, plays, movies, television programs, were considered only in terms of what they had to say, what they had to communicate in ideas. But experience was itself the communication, what the brain did. Man was oblivious to these changes. A story was a story—complete with plots, morals, points of view, and ultimate meanings—to fit within preestablished value systems. Considerations of story on the neural level are another story. Recent research has shown that the parts of the brain from which memories are evoked so easily and regularly are those we find most liable to exaggerated electrical discharge during flicker, and it is here too that in normal subjects the pattern of incoming stimuli can be seen abstracted and preserved for some time after the stimulation has ceased.

The movie experience is a flicker experience of a frequency of twenty-four times per second, slightly higher and safer than the level considered dangerous for certain brains. The reflection of projected light from a treated surface, a surface encompassing up to eighty per cent of the visual field, can have the effect on the neural level of an electronic brain message. Where is the meaning when we realize the emotional response is a function of the flicker experience reactivating memory imprints stored in the operant circuits of the brain? The implications of such a hypothesis are obvious. How can we merely discuss "I like it/I don't like it" without reference to questions about the brain's activity, a universe without I's.

Neural energy is not produced by the major receptors for sensory stimuli. The sources for neural energy are the gravitational receptors, the stretching-type muscles. The visual receptors, bringing in up to two-thirds of the sensory stimuli for the brain, are useless as a source of neural energy. In this light, look to the transaction between the environmental force and the organism in terms of the information provided to the brain. The visual receptors tend to pick up light as motion. The human eye has economically confined its best form and color vision to a relatively small fovea, while its perception of motion is better on the periphery. When peripheral vision has picked up some object conspicuous by brilliancy or light contrast or color, or above all by motion, there is reflex feedback to bring it into the fovea. . . . We tend to bring any object that attracts our attention into a standard position and orientation, so that the visual image which we form of it varies within as small a range as possible.

Consider the motion-picture experience not in terms of the images of the movie, but the motion of the flickering light, the flashing on and off, twenty-four times per second. A relationship can be established between the information this experience provides for the brain and the production of new quanta of neural energy. Unlike the usual situation where the eye scans one hundred per cent of the visual field, picks up motion, and brings it into the fovea, the light as motion of the movie experience can encompass up to eighty per cent of the visual field. The normal reflex feedback, bringing the movement into the fovea, is not possible, as the outer muscles are locked into a pattern of stretching activity quite unlike any other performed in the daily routine of contemporary life. The information from this experience is measured by what the brain does to adjust to the change. In this case there is every reason to speculate that the experience will provide a potent source of neural energy. The source is not in what the eye sees, but in what the eye is doing: the stretching of the muscles, the gravitational receptors, providing information for the brain.

These speculations on the relationship of the environmental force and the activity integrated on the neural level raise an interesting question. Going beyond the nonexistent linear construct of movie and into the direct experience of the brain, we can easily see that the very same movie, experienced in two different theaters, can provide the brain with significantly different information. Sitting to the rear of a theater with a postage-stamp screen will expose only about five to ten per cent of the visual field to light as motion. Sitting in the first few rows of a seventy mm. theater will expose up to eighty per cent of the visual field to light as motion. It appears obvious that the latter experience would be more intense on the neural level. But man, the nonexistent linear construct, could not get past the level of "What did it say?" "Was it good?" or "Was it bad?" His mind saw a movie; the experience in the present changed the way the brain worked.

Every movie is the first movie. Mechanisms for perceiving and responding to stimuli are at least partly generated by earlier stimulation. The information received by the brain both determines the manner of response and inhibits the establishment of new programs. The ability to apprehend the external world with freshness of perception commonly decreases as the mind and the senses become conditioned by repeated experiences. Human beings thus perceive the world, and respond to it, not through the whole spectrum of their genetic potentialities but only through the areas of this spectrum not blocked by inhibitory mechanisms and made functional by environmental influences, especially the early ones. The information received by the brain from the movie experience at once serves to encode and rigidify operant programs. This encoding and rigidification as information must be considered in terms of the continuous operations of the brain. There is reason to believe that information is stored in the brain by alteration of the storage elements. Once this change is effected, the information provided by the experience of new stimuli may be to activate the programs stored as alteration of the storage elements, giving form to extant operational patterns.

Certain programs have been coded into the brain's operation as species information. These patterns activate the orthosympathetic systems, part of the autonomic, or involuntary, muscular systems of the body. The orthosympathetic systems supply the energy for "flight or fight" responses by pumping adrenalin through the system. The hormonal changes necessary to perform the act are set in motion by the brain before the performance actually begins. Every movie is the first movie. The brain goes into its stereotyped movie program even before the ticket is purchased. The information received by the brain from the experience of purchasing a ticket may be enough to activate the hormonal responses of the movie experience. Buy your ticket: See the movie.

We can talk about information-patterning for the brain only in the present. There is no other universe for the brain, only the all-at-once universe of simultaneous operations. Every action performed is ever present, programmed into the operant patterns of the brain as information. That's all there is; there is no more. What's here's everywhere; what's not here's nowhere. All that is real can be found in the operations of the brain. Time and space are considerations of the interpretation of the ordering, and not of the transaction. Causality and sequence are myths. There is no first time. Sequence is simultaneity.

Man created his world and was molded by his use of it. Nature was a man-made phenomenon. The invention-realization of the nonlinear extension of the brain's experience—the socialization of mind—is on the same level as that of the invention of talking. Man did not realize he was talking until the day a man said, "We're talking." By understanding that the experience of the brain is continually communicated through the process of information, it can be seen that the extensions of man are to be viewed as communication, not as a means for the flow of communication. As such they provide the information for the continual process of neural coding. The interval is closed. No more individuals. No more man. It's a process. We construct a loop where output provides the information for input. On the species level the output (behavior) is environment. The input is the neural impulse. A change in environment (output) provides the brain with information it needs to maintain its continuity through adaptation, or a change in its operations (input). Man was the creator of "mind." Man determined his evolution. Man died. Dead and gone.

Dangers exist because the frames of reference which enable the deciphering of the patterns of communication are not easily understood. Man, living in a nonexistent illusory world of the past instant, could not readily discern the patterns of the activity of his brain. Change took place too rapidly. Man changed himself into non-existence. Man is dead.

A word from the author: It is not the easiest activity to escape the human race and then effect the destruction of mankind. Perhaps the death of an abstraction is the most difficult death. The brain is conditioned by the activity of an abstract way of thinking, by the information it receives. These patterns do not die easily. Their destruction is the ultimate violence. What remains is the ghostly dreamworld of man—a world, an abstraction, in which participation is no longer possible.

The brain tends to respond to new experiences in certain stereotyped ways. The prior responses to experiences determine response to new experience. There is a tendency for operational patterns to rigidify, inhibiting the acquisition of new experience. All coding, all neural imprinting, takes place in the present. The operational imprint can be said to be a measure of information, the adaptive change. This imprinting is continually happening. Man was never aware of it; he was never asked to give, and never gave, his consent to it. There was, there is, no choice.

The most important feature of the age of electric technology is the moving of information. This is not to be confused with words, images. It has to do with control, with the extension of the central nervous system outside the body, into the world as the world. New technologies effected a change in the operation of the brain. Telephone companies, electric companies, construction companies, hardware manufacturers, etc., were all in the same business: moving information. Telephone companies based charges on time; electricity companies charged for power; television manufacturers charged for a product. None of them based charges on information, on the evolutionary effect of their products and services upon mankind.

Electricity is the unitive factor that can make all brains in the world perform the same operations simultaneously. Through electronic technology, millions upon millions of brains can act on the same information at the same time. Information is a measure of a change in the brain's activity, a frequency modulation. Every brain working the same way, on the same frequency, the same wave length, performing the same operations simultaneously. Not brotherhood, but unity.

The past is illusion. The future is not. It is even necessary to stop talking of the present, which implies other aspects of the abstraction of time. Time, which cannot be directly experienced. Time, which does not exist in the neural world. Considerations of the interpretation of the ordering of the brain's experience pertain to the world of the past. The past is illusion. There is no sequence. There is no specific causation. There is only the ordering and arrangement of the experience of the brain in a universe of simultaneous operations. The past is illusion. Sequence is simultaneity.

The brain is a terminal machine in the process that is itself the dynamic, the reference point. This reference point is not to be found as a substantial basis, but in considerations of function and operations. It will be found in the process of transmission of neural pattern. It is through observation of operations, measurement of information, that this dynamic situation can be dealt with. Observation and measurement, not classification and categorization.

The brain is constantly synchronizing with new rhythms. As such it programs itself as a self-organizing system called evolution. This constant transaction with new rhythms and the ordering process is the level to which attention should now be applied. Not sex, not unconscious urges, not iconic archetypes, not metaphysics. There is no purpose. There are no goals.

Man always valued his identity, but knowing who he was proved only to tell him what had already happened. People are no longer important or worthy of any consideration. Man is dead. No more people, with their loves, fears, longings. It has been said that a man thinks he amounts to a great deal, but to a mosquito he is only something good to eat. Do not recognize people's feelings. Human feelings do not exist. Respect no one. People do not exist. No more dreams, no more illusion.

"I am in love." The neural impulse does not necessarily bear relationship to the sensory stimulus. Stereotyped neural programs can be activated in any number of different situations. "I am in love." Faces, bodies change but the same love remains, the same feeling. Such stereotyped programs are established by prior experience which both encodes and rigidifies the operant activities of the brain, delimiting the range of potential responses. "I am in love." All pleasures, all love exist in the brain. Neural programs. Not heart.

Every movie is the first movie. Every lover is the first love in terms of the simultaneous operations of the brain. The brain most likely has an operant circuit for the experience of orgasm. Whenever an appropriate partner happens along, the button is pressed . . . bzzz . . . the circuit is activated. The acquisition of experience by the brain inhibits acquisition of new experience. It is an ordering and rigidifying process. The bzzz activating the orgasm circuit gives form to what is already happening in the brain. The brain can set off this circuit with or without the active participation of the partner. Some of man's finest moments occurred when he was fast asleep. Bzzz. The neural impulse is not necessarily determined by the nature of the sensory input. Any variety of stimuli will do it. The explicit operations of the brain will one day be readily available at the press of a button.

Electrical stimulation of the brain has triggered experiences that cannot be distinguished as being different from real. In other words, the brain is not capable of distinguishing between the real and the illusory. By appropriate electrical stimulation of cell aggregates of living human brains, phenomena can be evoked which have reminiscent aspects (in some instances memorylike in the old sense of the term), characteristics which at times rival ordinary afferent sensory stimulation in their vivid insistence and intrusion upon the stream of consciousness, and at still other times rival effective responses appropriate to the content of the phenomenon elicited. For the brain, there is no illusion. Reality is whatever the brain is doing. Electrical stimulation can activate programs of prior experience. In the process of decoding and deciphering the functions of neural activity, it seems a realizable possibility to be able to enjoy such pleasures as the orgasm a hundred, a thousand times a day.

For the brain, there is no illusion. There is no line marking arbitrary divisions such as good and bad, normal and perverse, sanity and insanity. Reality is whatever the brain is doing. On the neural level there is no insanity, there is no negative mode of thought, there is no perversion, there are no impossibilities, no responsibilities.

Given that the genetic structure of the organism stabilized ages ago, man's evolutionary growth and development became a function of his own activities. Information passed through generations of brains. The effect of this information is environment. Environment is past experience; environment is illusion. The environment included man. Man never knew what was happening. His knowledge, his awareness, was illusion. To ask questions, to decode, to decipher the transactions, look to the environment, the effect, and work backward. The efferent motor activity, the output, or environment, related by feedback of information to the afferent neural impulse, the input. Forget about man. The brain is only a terminal, not an originator. Look to the environment and measure how the brain changes through the transaction with the forces that are non-linear extensions of its own experience.

The brain is not a repository for ideas. No brain ever had an idea in it. Realize, then, that man molded himself, and that nature was therefore man-made, reality being in the operations of the brain. All things considered to be innate and natural were in effect functions of the ordering of the simultaneous operations of the brain. The key to nature lies in the study of man's communication. Man, the most social of animals. The Golden Rule said, "Do unto others." But there is no "other." There is no self. The division is gone. There is unlimited involvement.

In the name of God. And God created man in His own image. And man created God in his own image. But now the only image to be considered is operant, one which cannot statically exist in a fixed place. It is to be located in the operations of the brain, not in a place, not in a time. Space and time, which cannot be directly experienced. In the universe of simultaneous operations there is only information. Man was not aware of direct experience. These dimensions are beyond space and time. They are the dimensions of direct experience, dimensions not accessible to the individual mind, not accessible to man.

Did man evolve into God? Being everywhere, every time, in the universe of simultaneous operations? Where man went, so went man's information. The physical transportation of man became trivial compared to the transmission of information beyond space and time. Man-made technology changed the way every brain works. The understanding of how the brain orders its operant imaging processes created gods out of men. But there is only the universe of simultaneous neural functions. What of gods? No time for them, no space for them anymore.

No more art, no more artists. Actions, not objects. Ritual, not possessions. The real artistry is in deciphering the process of neural coding. This navigation threads the way through the clues strewn around the environment and sets processes in motion to allow patterns to reveal themselves.

This exercise is not dealing with ultimate definitions. It is presenting hypotheses that are to be used only so long as they are functional. Any hypothesis is limited by its parameters. For any system there is a truth proving the system which cannot be shown to be true within the system. For man this was the ordering of the brain by direct nonlinear experience, which man interpreted as consciousness—the consciousness that could never say how it became conscious. Ideas never reveal what the brain is doing. There is no consciousness, no unconsciousness. There is only what the brain is doing. But since this is known only in terms of an ordering of the brain, a transaction not accessible to the individual in question, the system goes beyond the individual brain and into the evolutionary process, where the activities of a multiplicity of brains serve as terminals for a continuous flow of information. For every system there is a truism proving the system which cannot be shown to be true within the system. Man is dead.

Man is dead. The dying, the death, was self-awareness, self-consciousness, self-esteem. It's a myth. It's over with. Man sought self-expression, individuality, personality. But his image of the world was a function of the experience of his brain. The brain is capable only of acting on information within the parameters of its construction. It is not a "free agent." What must be analyzed is the process, the operant concept of what something is doing, rather than static, fixed states of being. Considerations of individuality and personality only beg the pertinent questions.

The notion of freedom is simply absurd. Where there is no choice, there is no freedom. Antagonists, protagonists. Illusory abstractions. All functions of similar operant brain-imaging. Me and you, we and they, good and bad, subject and object. Antagonists and protagonists: It's all a question of self-identity, of ownership. Ownership of ideas.

It is no longer possible to relate to political considerations—a province of man, the illusory past. Democracy, communism, socialism, fascism: all gone. Liberty, freedom, police states, welfare states: all gone. Beyond freedom. Man was never free. He was a prisoner of his biophysiological functions. He acted in terms of the construction of the brain and the information it received. The information that was received without consent or awareness. The notion of free man, the notion of individual choice, is no longer valid.

Political considerations are trivial. The leaders of governments throughout the world thought in terms of control, believing power to be the key. But there is always complete control: Information is the key. The direct nonlinear experience of the brain is communicable. Information passes across the arbitrary boundaries of mankind as though they never existed.

The so-called emotional states of man were nothing more than habit. Fear. Love. Longing. Hate. Pain. Pleasure. Joy. Press the button, and the brain will activate the program. So too with man's noblest feelings. Dignity. Honor. Altruism. Patriotism. Habit. The human habit.

There is no choice with information. It is a measure of effect, a measure of the change in the brain's operations. As the brain functions in a universe of continuous, simultaneous operations, it may be said information is always circulating in the system. As information is a measure of control, there is always one hundred per cent control. There is no choice.

It is interesting to note that research into the activity of the brain shows that the program of operations in terms of direct experience becomes imprinted as an operant circuit. It must be remembered that the operation of the brain is activity of which one cannot be aware. These imprints exist in the simultaneous universe of operations. It has been demonstrated through electronic stimulation of the temporal lobe by implanted electrodes that the imprint of a previous program can become activated. Illusions of familiarity of a *déjà vu* nature, as well as interpretation of shape, clearness, and speed, are activated by stimulation of the temporal cortex and subsequent electrical discharge on only one side of the brain, the side responsible for minor-handedness. We also know that the flicker experience of a frequency of that of a movie (twenty-four frames per second) could excite this same area of the brain through exaggerated electrical discharge. Considerations of individual "mind" only beg questions that may be readily explored through analysis and observation on the operant level. Operant observations and analysis are impossible within the abstraction system of man.

Discern the patterns by measuring output and relating it to input. How a change in the environment is related to a change in the brain's operation. The relationship is nonlinear; the measure of the relationship is information, a measure of the change of the brain's operations. It goes beyond the abstraction of the individual. In a way man could not see, he was animated by his extensions. He was the terminal, not the originator. It all went through him. It wasn't life; it was process.

It comes down to rhythms. Reality is to be found in the process of neural activity. Systems of abstraction are developed which allow the functioning phenomena to monitor their own activities. This monitoring, rather than being an observation of extant activity, is actually new activity. It is represented by frequencies, rhythms, numbers. When man tried to find the ultimate material basis of identity, he got down to the level of molecular spectra, only to find neither materials nor mechanisms, but a self-organizing pattern of frequencies. A process. A whole which can be represented by operant mathematical symbols, but which can be talked about and measured only in terms of effect. Who am I?

There are not, there will not be, any footnotes in the body of this exercise. Ownership is a human habit. The author presents not ideas, but information. Not words and images, but a transaction that can be measured only in terms of information. It may appear inconsistent to use the linear format of the printed book to convey the message that there is only information. The entity "book" is an arbitrary representation of reality, not dissimilar to symbolizing operant patterning as "man." On the neural level we can see how "book," an extension of man, fed back signals telling the brain what to do. There is a sense in which we can say that there is communication of information between man and his products. This is process. It is integrated on the neural level. It is nonlinear.

Language. This exercise is using language to say that language does not exist. There is only information controlling the direct experience of the brain. The currency of the nervous system is the neural impulse. The key to language is to be found in the operations of the brain. The universals of language are the universals of neural patterns. Different languages cut up reality in terms of their own bias. Mathematics must be included in this consideration as a language. However, it may even be in the cards that there is no such thing as "Language" (with a capital *L*) at all! The statement that "thinking is a matter of language" is an incorrect generalization of the more nearly correct idea that "thinking is a matter of different tongues." The different tongues are the real phenomena and may generalize down not to any such universal as "Language," but to something better called "sublinguistic" or "superlinguistic"—and NOT ALTOGETHER unlike, even if much unlike, what we now call "mental."

The trap is in the concept "language." Whatever is happening can be considered perfectly well without ever using the conceptual framework of "language," which by its nature makes it difficult to consider the transaction, the process. We are not concerned with the linear system of "man and man's language," but with experience on the neural level, the only direct experience. Words are not directly experienced. Man never experienced words. He experienced another man talking, radios, books, televisions, telephones, etc. The experience was never that of language. We move from the relationship of man-man talking, man-radio, man-book, man-man thinking, to a study of the transacting process that can be considered in unambiguous, numerical terms when dealt with on the level of operant, neural activity. Yet this exercise uses words. When we talk about reality we never start at the beginning and we use concepts more accurately defined only by their application. It's part of the process. The author is aware that for every system capable of producing a logical truth, there is a truism proving the system which cannot be shown to be true within the system.

Reality is not words, not the construct of language. Reality is in the nonlinear function of neural activity. The only real phenomena are operant and nonlinear. Words can be considered only in terms of the illusory past. Man thought the choice was between ideas that were expressed through language. The choice for man really concerned information, how the usage of various language patterns would change the way the brain worked. Since man could never be aware of the activity of his brain, there was no choice. Silence.

Real control had nothing to do with the kind of control exercised by national governments. Control is through the process of information. Man's technologies, viewed as communication, as feedback extensions, relayed back signals telling the brain what to do. While governments exercised their traditional prerogatives, the process continued unnoticed. No democratic populace, no legislative body, ever indicated by choice, by vote, what kind of information was desired. Nobody ever voted for the telephone. Nobody ever voted for the automobile. Nobody ever voted for printing. Nobody ever voted for television. Nobody ever voted for space travel. Nobody ever voted for electricity. Nobody ever voted for nuclear power.

There are only nonlinear phenomena. The communication of direct neural experience is an invention more important than the wheel, the steam engine, nuclear energy. The trip through the internal mappings of the nervous system is far more exciting, far more important, and far more dangerous than the journey to the moon, and the farthest reaches of outer space.

It is a question of searching for questions. This exercise is not setting forth rules or formulating dogma. It is an attempt to create a working model, not with an eye to truth but to convenience. The only rules applicable are those that are convenient to use. In this system there is no interest in, there is no possibility of, truth. There is no longer a solid base, a substantial reality, from which to make pronouncements. We move toward an always inferred, unknowable reality with the symbols, the frames of reference, available to us. What we find is only a model. Man was such a model. Man, the model, is dead.

It is no longer necessary to say yes to life. No one is there to listen; no one is interested in you, no one is interested in your words.

II

No man's land.

Progress is merely decreation. *Entia non sunt multiplicanda praeter necessitatem.* We must not assume the existence of any entity until we are compelled to do so. This principle is purely destructive, it takes something away. Decreation: A person can doubt only if he has learned certain things; as he can miscalculate only if he has learned to calculate. The advances of civilization are gross exaggerations; a function of the language with its built-in commitment to the accretive historical model. Flat earth: round earth. It isn't a one hundred per cent accretive advance from one to two: one hundred assumes and decreates ninety-nine. Round earth assumes and decreates flat earth. Invisible assumes and decreates visible. Events assume and decreate matter. The relativistic universe assumes and decreates the mechanistic universe. Progress is always a transcendence of what is obvious: decreation. Is it simply that progress in any aspect is a movement through changes of terminology?

A no man's land, or better said, a no signals region extends between past and future. Universe is finite: no space-time continuum. A voice out of the past? The reliving of an experience? Don't call it memory. Is it possible to remember? A seeing into the past? It does not show us the past. Anymore than our senses show us the present. Nor can it be said to communicate the past to us.

Universe is finite: a process of decreation: the passing of the created into the uncreated. Decreation: the created passes into man-made invention. Reality passes into description.

The end of the waste system. The waste: the generalizations of previous epochs. Decreation: getting through the history of words. We must not assume the existence of any entity until we are compelled to do so. The point is that unnecessary units in a sign language mean nothing.

The accretive principle: the predominant way people live, like the old-fashioned idea of making a living; amounting to something. Stuff starts at one point and goes through accretive increments of time, of space, of history, etc., to get to another point. Universe: no accretion; no accumulation; no development; no continuity. Neither before nor after; neither behind nor beyond; neither here nor there; neither inside nor outside; neither from nor to: No direction; no between: no communication.

Universe: a verb. Not existing in time, but time itself and not the time of past, present, future. Time undifferentiated in activity, not time of being. Universe: a decreated world: a moment in time/and of time./ A moment not out of time, but in time, in what we call history:/ transecting, bisecting the world of time, a moment in time/ but not like a moment of time,/ A moment in time but time was made through that moment:/ for without the meaning there is no time, and that moment/ of time gave the meaning.

Awkwardness: The only way to fit the uniqueness of insights into current laws. Awkwardness: stymied by perception, by knowledge. Awkwardness: the primary advantage thus gained is that experience is not interrogated with the benumbing repression of common sense.

Universe is finite: objectified expression of activity: the assumption of the positive-negative abstractions particular to the subject-predicate proposition; the assumption of the process of subject-predicate. No ultimate subject: the unity is unitless. Where you end/ And I begin/ Or any else, in fine,/ On such dichotomies depend/ There's no one left to draw a line. Subject-predicate: noun'd. Noun: negated. Syntax: confused.

A noun is the name of things . . . why after a thing is named write about it. The major accomplishment of science is that it has never produced an objective fact, never proven the existence of an object. No nouns: no objects, no people, no propositions, nothing. Living with the growing terror of nothing to think about.

Undifferentiation of activity: no division of activity into parts. No differences; no between. To be without description of to be.

It is impossible to pay less than one hundred per cent attention. It is impossible to do less than you do. Universe: verb. Do: always one hundred per cent: the do of do; the do of not do. Activity: always one hundred per cent: the activity of activity; the activity of nonactivity. Experience: always one hundred per cent: the experience of experiencing; the experience of not experiencing. You can't do less than you do. Doing: complete, obligatory, always one hundred per cent, whether the focus is the part or the whole; the totality or the selection obscuring the totality. "I am" is doing: don't call it being. "I am not" is doing: don't call it nonexistence. "I think" is doing: don't call it thought. Do: The final elegance, not to console/ Nor sanctify, but plainly to propound.

Undifferentiated activity. Don't call it Life. Don't call it Man. Talk of gods and man destroyed, the right/ To know established as the right to be./ The ancient symbols will be nothing then./ We shall have gone behind the symbols/ To that which they symbolized. Use unambiguous language for objective description: elementary physical laws are all expressed by statistical formulas. All the pictures which science now draws of nature, and which alone seem capable of according with observational fact, are mathematical pictures.

The description is the thing. The most important thing is the next word; the to-be-said. Not a word and yet another kind of word: a refinement of general language, supplementing it with appropriate tools to represent relations for which ordinary verbal expression is imprecise or cumbersome. No ultimate subject. Just by avoiding the reference to the conscious subject which infiltrates daily language, the use of mathematical symbols secures the unambiguity of definition required for objective description.

Get through the history of words. Throw away the lights, the definitions,/ And say of what you see in the dark/ That it is this or that it is that,/ But do not use the rotted names.

Universe: verb. The coupling of observer-observed system. The doing of man-environment. The doing of "I think." Universe: not observer, not man, not I. The unity is unitless, an expression of undifferentiated activity. We need no longer discuss whether light consists of particles or waves; we know all there is to be known if we have found a mathematical formula which accurately describes its behavior and we can think of it as either particles or waves according to our mood and convenience of the moment. It exists in a mathematical formula; this, and nothing else, expresses the ultimate reality.

Our task can only be to aim at communicating experiences and views to others by means of language in which the practical use of every word stands in complementary relation to attempts at its strict definition. This exercise sets forth exact notions with the inexact language of the spurious names and generalizations that have crept into the language as truth. There's no other way. There are no precisely stated axiomatic certainties from which to start. There is not even the language in which to frame them. The only possible procedure is to start from verbal expressions which when taken by themselves with the current meanings of their words are ill-defined and ambiguous. Welcome the contradictions, welcome the confusion . . . as you would success.

The coupling of observer-observed system is finite. The observation, the measuring operation, is irreversible. The real world measured itself out of existence. The model need not be that of an objective, immovable world around us. Philosophers of our time cannot ignore the fact that interaction between observer and observed is finite and cannot be made as small as desired. Observation and perturbation inevitably go together and the world around us is in perpetual flux, because we observe it.

A physical quantity must not be defined by verbal reduction to other familiar conceptions, but by prescribing the operations necessary to produce and measure it. Universe is finite: decreation of the outside world, independent of us; decreation of the outside world not directly accessible to us. The description is the thing. The description: a mathematical formulation, the statistical expression of coupling. The making of models or pictures to explain mathematical formulae and the phenomena they describe is not a step toward, but a step away from reality. Universe is finite: not a word, and yet another kind of word; and the word must be the thing it represents.

No nouns: the notion of an actual entity as the unchanging subject of change is completely abandoned. The unity is unitless: An actual entity is at once the subject experiencing and the superject of its experiences. It is subject-superject and neither half of this description can for a moment be lost sight of. Unitless unity: the negation of one. Unitless unity: the operation, the statistical expression of coupling, of activity. Unitless unity: The poet and his subject are inseparable. There is no ultimate subject. Before the birth of Doubt/ We–you and I–were one,/ Who now, alack,/ Are both undone!

To measure is to disturb. We used to imagine that there was a real universe, outside of us, which could persist even when we stopped observing it. The negation of the empirical notion of antecedent observation: we can never catch the world taking a holiday. Observation and perturbation inevitably go together and the method of pinning down thought to the strict systematization of detailed discrimination, already effected by antecedent observation, breaks down. Each observation destroys the bit of the universe observed, and so supplies knowledge only of a universe which has already become past history. We cannot abstract ourselves from the world. We form together with it, an inseparable whole. There are no actors and spectators, but a mixed crowd . . . reject, absolutely renounce the idea of an objective real world. The concern is with our observation of nature, and not nature itself.

Description is the thing. Decreation of the idealized real world, the thing world, the people world. Experiments are the only elements which really count. Coupling of observer-observed, an event: the matter of fact. The elementary particles themselves are not as real; they form a world of potentialities or possibilities rather than of things and facts. Physical phenomena: not things made of matter. Coupling: the matter of fact. Do not look behind the facts since the facts themselves make up the doctrine. Physical phenomena: coupling: the matter of fact. To confront fact in its total bleakness is for any poet a completely baffling experience. Reality is not the thing but the aspect of the thing.

Unnecessary units in a language mean nothing. The unnecessary unit: an invention. The real world: an invention. Invention: a question of decreation. Invention: a question of realization, not intention. We must not assume the existence of any entity until we are compelled to do so. We approach a society/ Without a society. We are compelled to assume the existence of an entity only by decreating that entity. Invention by decreation.

Concepts are the impersonal effect of an epoch. Names are included in conceptual exercises either to impress the reader or to support a notion so weak as to require a name with which to tyrannize the reader. The first idea was not our own. Not one idea in this exercise is original. They are the ideas of the reader, not the author. There is no author. Not one idea in this exercise is original.

The final elegance: assuming, asking the question. No answers. No explanations. Why do you demand explanations? If they are given, you will once more be facing a terminus. They cannot get you any further than you are at present. The solution: not an explanation: a description and knowing how to consider it.

Everything has been explained. There is nothing left to consider. The explanation can no longer be treated as a definition. The question: a description. The answer: not explanation, but a description and knowing how to consider it. Asking or telling: there isn't any difference.

Why is a contradiction more to be feared than a tautology? Success in this exercise is confusion. Knowledge is tautological. Knowledge is the thing you know and how can you know more than you do know. The decreation of reality: as it is known; as it is not known. The decreation of reality: the invention of reality.

Make or do: You can't do other than do. Each observation destroys the bit of the universe observed, and thus supplies knowledge only of a universe which has already become past history. Make-create: spurious conceptions of the empirical notion of antecedent observation. Make-create: accretive advance from nothing to made; from nothing to created; from nothing to thing. Make-create: a real world taking a holiday. You can't do other than do. Doing: do. Not doing: do. Make-create: do. Not making-not creating: do. Observation and perturbation inevitably go together and the world around us is in perpetual flux, because we observe it. You can't do other than do.

Nothing comes before performance.

Concepts which refer to distinctions beyond possible experience have no physical meaning and ought to be eliminated. This principle should be applied to the idea of physical continuity. No nature at an instant. An infinitely small distance cannot be measured . . . we should especially emphasize the impossibility of physically defining a continuum in space and time. No accretion. It is impossible to locate a thing, stuff, etc., in space at an instant of time. No pictures. Experiments, measurements are what count. These events must be treated as the fundamental objective constituents . . . an analysis in terms of doings or happenings. No nature at an instant. Nature is such that it is impossible to determine absolute motion by any experiment whatsoever. No nature at an instant: no movement; no change; no distance; no speed; no development; no continuity; no creation; no from; no direction; no there; no before; no accretion.

No nature at an instant. But what can be described can also happen: the description is the thing. Where was it one first heard of the truth? The the.

The past has another pattern and ceases to be a mere sequence—/ Or even development. No accretive time: a unique seriality of incremental creative advance. Physical phenomena cannot be represented in the accretive space-time continuum. No nature at an instant: no pictures: no mirrors. No pictorial interpretation on accustomed lines, but establishing relations between observations. These relations are represented statistically. Their expression, a consequence of the coupling of observer-observed is independent of time and place; independent of development; independent of seriality.

Measurements, experiments are what count: nonaccretive discrete energy values for discrete states (S) of experience. The measurement (S) destroys the bit of the universe observed. Observation and perturbation inevitably go together and "the world around us" is in perpetual flux because we observe it. No accretive states of experience: S2+S3+S4, etc. To measure is to disturb. Every measurement is S1. There is no S2. There can be no addition, no comparison, no creation, no reproduction, no difference. A no signals region extends between past and future. One picture of the scenario about the caterpillar stage does not communicate its transformation into the butterfly stage. No signals region: no difference. No accretive states of experience.

The end of the beginning, of first, of last, of before or after, of between. A no-signals region extends between past and future: no man's land.

It isn't necessary to be aware of concepts in order to live them. Knowledge makes no difference: measurements are what count. Knowledge makes no difference: to know is to measure.

The doing of "you do." I, you, she, he, they, represent the concept of the static unchanging subject of change, advancing through accretive states of experience in a space-time continuum. There's nothing for you to do. Do I dare to eat a peach?

I: a noun. I am: noun'd. Existence is being: noun'd. To be or not to be: noun'd. Universe is finite: negation of the noun: no things: nothing.

Coupling: irreversible: noninterchangeable. If you came this way,/ Taking any route, starting from anywhere,/ At any time or at any season,/ It would always be the same: you would have to put off/ Sense and notion. You are not here to verify,/ Instruct yourself, or inform curiosity/ or carry report.

Coupling of observer-observed system is finite: the observational process is irreversible. Physical knowledge is of an observational nature, in the sense that each item is an assertion of the results of an observation, actual or hypothetical. The study of coupling between observer and observed system, between man and physics, will probably oblige us to revise the notion of value and to dissociate it from that of scarcity. Value is in activity. Physical phenomena: a verb. Value is not to be found in scarcity of people, things, ideas, etc. Physical phenomena: the irreversible coupling: a verb. Only the final sum matters. The computation assumes the history of the system in its expression. Physical science consists of purely structural knowledge, so that we know only the structure of the universe which it describes. For strict expression of physical knowledge a mathematical form is essential, because it is the only way in which we can confine its assertions to structural knowledge. Every path to knowledge of what lies beneath the structure is then blocked by an impenetrable mathematical symbol.

People world: things, objects, knowledge, ideas. Universe: And say of what you see in the dark/ That it is this or that it is that/ But do not use the rotted names.

"I think," or "I do not think": syncategorematic: cannot be used as terms in themselves. The finite, irreversibility of coupling cannot be ignored. It does not take finding to show what we were looking for, and fulfillment of a wish to show what we wanted. It is not the expected thing that is the fulfillment, but rather: its coming about. The mistake is deeply rooted in our language. Universe is finite: at once both subject and predicate of conventional language. The word that must be said, that can't be said: not a word and yet another kind of word, that hallowed and accursed word which is life and death at the same time. Universe is finite: a form to speak the word/ And every latent double in the word.

Our knowledge has led us to this place: nowhere. Our knowledge has proven one thing: nothing.

It's a question of getting through the history of words: the spurious conceptions, generalizations: the rotted names. Is it peace,/ Is it a philosopher's honeymoon, one finds/ On the dump?

The experience of not having an experience: Everything is interchangeable on a live level. Undifferentiation of activity: communication is a myth: here to there; you to me; then to now; nothing to something. Everything is interchangeable on a live level.

Experience a minute. Experience an hour. Can you experience a minute and an hour together, simultaneously, at the same time? This is an important question to ask.

It is very noteworthy that what goes on in thinking practically never interests us. The concern is always with thoughts . . . not thinking. "I see" . . . "I know" . . . "I perceive": syncategorematic: cannot be used as terms in themselves. They are noun'd.

Everything is interchangeable on a live level. Can I think away the impression of familiarity where it exists; and think it into a situation where it does not?

Indeterminacy: interchangeability. The actual occasions, the coupling of observer-observed, are devoid of all indetermination. Potentiality has passed into realization. They are complete and determinate matter of fact, devoid of all indecision. They form the ground of obligation. The concepts of the people world, the thing world: indeterminate: interchangeable. Universe: determinate; noninterchangeable; irreversible.

People world, thing world concepts: syncategorematic: cannot be used as terms in themselves. They are noun'd. Such terms express the definiteness of the actuality in question, but their own natures do not in themselves disclose in what actual entities, what coupling operation, this potentiality of ingression is realized. Actual entity: coupling: noninterchangeable: irreversible. Syncategorematic terms: decreated. Me? I don't.

Nothing left to say. Any absolute statement relating to properties of the world around us must be considered as an unjustified extrapolation. Only a description based on observations and relative to the process of observation can be valid. We no longer talk of states; we measure. The measuring operation: irreversible and indeterminate.

Living with nothing: costing not less than everything. Do I dare/ Disturb the universe? Living with the knowledge that intention makes no difference. In the oblivion of cards/ One exists among pure principles./ Neither the cards nor the trees nor the air/ Persist as facts. This is an escape/ To principium, to meditation./ One knows at last what to think about/ And thinks about it without consciousness,/ Under the oak trees, completely released.

There is no difference in doing less. You can't pay less than one hundred per cent attention. There's no quantity in a no thing, non-accretive dimension. Numbers don't count, from one to two. Quantity: ha ha. The doing of "you do," the doing of "you don't": one hundred per cent attention. The name, the sign of distinction, the description are assumed as a consequence of the coupling: undifferentiated activity; coupling: a verb. You can't pay less than one hundred per cent attention: call this a part, call that a whole; call this man, call that God; call this finite, call that infinite; call this the totality, call that the selection obscuring the totality: the description is the thing. The assumption of the description: a consequence of coupling: the observational operation: complete, determinate, one hundred per cent. You can't pay less than one hundred per cent attention. The part/ Is the equal of the whole. Everything is interchangeable on a live level.

Awareness no longer matters. Knowledge makes no difference: there is no outside world to change. There can't be communication if there are no differences: here and there, before and after, now and then. From and to are no longer useful words. Between is merely ridiculous.

There can't be communication if there is no differentiation: point A and point B. No differentiation: no communication. No differentiation: no signal accretively advancing by increments of space and time from message source A to message destination B. The current word is nonaccretive, undifferentiated, mathematical: the statistical expression of coupling: only the final sum matters: no communication.

Negation of the accretion principle. There is a prevalent misconception that "becoming" involves the notion of a unique seriality for its advance into novelty. This is the classic notion of time, which philosophy took over from common sense. There is a becoming of continuity but no continuity of becoming. No accretion: put off sense and notion. This is the springtime/ But not in time's covenant./ / Where is the summer, the unimaginable/ Zero summer? Spring-time: not in time's covenant. Space-time: not in time's covenant.

No end, no beginning. No matter how often what happened had happened any time any one told anything there was no repetition. No repetition, no competition, no emulation, no comparison, no meaning. This doesn't compete with that. This can't be a repetition of this.

Coupling produces finite interaction: the universe is finite. No mirrors, no pictures. To measure is to disturb. The measurement: the coupling: the matter of fact of physical phenomena: a statistical expression, the consequence of an event which is independent of time and place. There are no clocks, no mirrors, no place. There is no one to talk to. To live is to forget. Feign then what's by a decent tact believed/ And act that state is only so conceived,/ And build an edifice to form/ For house where phantoms may keep warm./ Imagine, then, by miracle, with me,/ (Ambiguous gifts, as what gods give must be)/ What could not possibly be there,/ And learn a style from a despair.

Universe: Physical experiments have found no solids, no continuous surfaces or lines—only discontinuous constellations of individual events. An aggregate of finites is finite. Therefore, universe as experientially defined, including both the physical and metaphysical, is finite.

Universe: a description. All physics one tautology;/ If you describe things with the right tensors/ All law becomes the fact that they can be described with them;/ This is the Assumption of the description. Assumption of the description: decreation of the thing described. Assumption of the description: the compulsion to assume the existence of an entity. By decreating we invent the existing entity; invent the unnecessary unit in a language; invent history; invent universe; invent reality, nature, etc. The decreation of the thing described compels us to assume the description of the thing described. Activity is undifferentiable: the names, the signs of distinction, the descriptions, are a consequence of the event, the coupling operation. Progress so far has consisted not so much in specifying what is actually observed, as in eliminating what is definitely unobserved and unobservable: the assumption of the description: decreation of the thing described. We approach a society/ Without a society.

Most men find the final dissolution of the universe as distasteful a thought as the dissolution of their own personality, and man's strivings after personal immortality have their macroscopic counterpart in these more sophisticated strivings after an imperishable universe. The universe is finite: there is nothing beyond, nothing outside this finiteness. Just the next measurement, the next word.

No explanation, no solution, but consideration of the question. Every proposition proposing a fact must in its complete analysis propose the general character of the universe required for the fact. The description, the proposition: not a definition, but a commission. Understanding a commission means: knowing what one has got to do.

The final truth about a phenomenon resides in the mathematical description of it. We go beyond the mathematical formula at our own risk; we may find a model or picture helps us to understand it, but we have no right to expect this and our failure to find such a model or picture need not indicate that either our reasoning or our knowledge is at fault. The description is the thing: Description is revelation. It is not/ The thing described, nor false facsimile. Nothing to describe.

Intention embarrasses. Every phrase and every sentence is an end and a beginning./ Every poem an epitaph. And any action/ Is a step to the block. Hope? But hope would be hope for the wrong thing. Love? But love would be love of the wrong thing. Stopping or starting: intention embarrasses.

Names: the description is the thing; the word must be the thing it represents; the most important thing is the next word. Getting through the history of words: Throw away the lights, the definitions,/ And say of what you see in the dark/ That it is this or that it is that/ But do not use the rotted names: mind, space, time, people, place, life, death, world.

Awkwardness: the only way to bear so much reality. Camouflage: the only way to live on the sophisticated edge of awareness. Confusion: the only way to live with the trivia of daily life.

Fact: doing. Fact: events. No nature at an instant. Activity: the matter of fact. The exquisite environment of fact. The final poem will be the poem of fact in the language of fact. But it will be the poem of fact not realized before.

Facts smirk.

Waste time: the thing world, the people world. Waste time: the trivia of daily life: the forms which command attention, respect. Waste time: the belief that idealization is above performance. Waste time: Ridiculous the waste sad time/ Stretching before and after. Waste time: Hill, cloud, field, wall . . ./ All that we touch, see, think . . ./ Unliven all: the stone, the dust/ The Earth itself and man and Man/ Turn thing/ And must. The incredible something of nothing.

No differentiation: Anybody can be interested in what anybody does but does that make any difference, is it all important. Anybody can be interested in what anybody says, but does that make any difference, is it at all important.

Forget, forget . . . Forget what you forget./ The diary entry: name, fact, place, and date/ Let go and let the loitering dead be dead. Universe is finite: obligatory, devoid of indecision, determinate. Will, doubt, desire, thought . . ./ All in us: / Faith, Hope, Love . . ./ Naught but THINGS itself away/ And you, and I, as meant, obey: / Are noun'd/ To naught. The incredible something of nothing: Still missing it though: / Though what, none know.

No accretion: no hierarchical order. There cannot be a hierarchy of the forms of elementary propositions. We can foresee only what we ourselves construct. Praise-blame: no hierarchical judgment. You are not to blame: what does this do to this. People do not help people: what does this do for this. No accretion: no hierarchical order. There cannot be a higher intelligence whether alien, technological, etc., for what cannot be expressed we do not express, what cannot be known we do not know. Judgment is impossible. No hierarchical order: Nature is never more complicated than we imagine it.

Numbers don't count. A multiplicity merely enters into the process through its individual members. Counting: comparison: one for a; two for b; There is no comparison. No accretion: no hierarchies. The description is the thing. No multiplicities: It is the chord that falsifies. Numbers don't count. A man and a woman/ Are one./ A man and a woman and a blackbird/ Are one. Numbers don't count. No one: unitless unity. Not a number, but a commission. Not a word and yet another kind of word.

Living with the growing terror of nothing to think about. Not a persistent thing with varying states, but a system of interrelated events. The old solidarity is gone, and with it the characteristics that, to the materialist, made matter seem more real than fleeting thoughts. The incredible something of nothing. Matter of solid objects and hard particles has no existence in reality and only appears to exist through our observing nonmaterial things in a confused way—through the bias of human spectacles.

No language can be anything but elliptical, requiring a leap of the imagination to understand its meaning in its relevance to immediate experience. Take the available language with its ambiguities and use it. The language is completely elastic. Anything can be said. Welcome the confusion: welcome the contradictions. Knowledge, wisdom, are a dead end. You can't know any more than you do know. Ask the fool.

Physical knowledge: observational: each item an assertion of the results of an observation. The coupling of observer-observed: undifferentiated activity. No difference: the duality of choice becomes the singularity of existence;/The effort of virtue the unconsciousness of foreknowledge. No distinctions: life-death; real-apparent; actual-hypothetical; no distinctions: true-false-maybe. No distinctions: past-present-future; end-beginning. Life is just a question of whatever you get away with.

The only place left is nowhere. So which way's which is now no more a query/ And up or down's as free as heads or tails./ Without a center or a pull to check it/ The very sense of that dimension fails: / Rise! Fall! Sink-swim? All idle theory.

Waiting for the present.

Things fall apart. No other to fight. No cause for which to struggle. No ideal for which to offer sacrifice. You are a metaphor and they are lies. And I . . . Not mine this life that must be lived in me. No other. No self. No man's land. Do you look into yourself in order to recognize the fury in his face? It is there as clearly as in your own breast. No one: the unity is unitless. One beats and beats for that which one believes,/ That's what one wants to get near. Could it after all/ Be merely oneself? The unity is unitless.

Don't try to repeal circumstances. Try something new. A people without history/ Is not redeemed from time, for history is a pattern/ Of timeless moments. Ahistory: Amen.

All time is eternally present. Not in the past, future, or present. Not before or after. Not now, then or when. Not anywhere. Here and there does not matter/ We must be still and still moving/ Into another intensity/ For a further union, a deeper communion.

The composition we live in changes but essentially what happens does not change. We inside us do not change but our emphasis and the moment in which we live changes. That it is never the same moment it is never the same emphasis at any successive moment of existing. Then really what is repetition? It is very interesting to ask and it is a very interesting thing to know. What is repetition? What is insistence? What is repetition? What is insistence? What is repetition? What is insistence?

The theory of description matters most./ It is the theory of the word for those/ For whom the word is the making of the world. Description is the thing: nothing.

Confusion: no-thing=thing. The incredible something of nothing.

Things operate the waste system. Idealization or performance: Ridiculous the waste sad time/ Stretching before and after. Activity is undifferentiable: no difference: no between. The performance decreates the idealization, the thing. And yet . . . the description of performance is itself an idealization, a thing. Confusion: we had the experience but missed the meaning,/ And approach to the meaning restores the experience/ In a different form, beyond any meaning.

The empirical: knowledge derived from experience. The epistemological: investigation of the methods and limits of knowledge. At the intersection of the empirical and the epistemological: a convenient nowhere, anytime, to be or not to be. Confusion: the incredible something of nothing. Beyond the reality principle there is nothingness: the void. And beyond the void: description of the void: the idealization, the objectification of nothing. Description of nothing, of event, of process, of doing, of void: a thing. The description is the thing. At the intersection of the empirical and the epistemological: a convenient nowhere, anytime, to be or not to be.

There is only a limited value/ In the knowledge derived from experience./ The knowledge imposes a pattern, and falsifies,/ For the pattern is new in every moment/ And every moment is a new and shocking/ Valuation of all we have been. At the intersection of the empirical and the epistemological: the first time that says anytime; the first place that says nowhere; the first thing that says nothing: the fact with a sense of humor.

Truth is now a matter of convenience; concepts are valid only in their capacity to sustain interest: only in their use. The interchangeability of concepts is a consequence of the noninterchangeability of the coupling operation. The description of the coupling, of the undifferentiated activity: a thing, a distinction, a differentiation. An instrument which would depict the Source/ Does not produce what baffles it as well. The description is the thing: everything. It is not a case of different ways of putting the same thing. Life consists/ Of propositions about life. It's the next word that matters. That one word might be a name, the release from a name.

The round earth followed from the flat earth. Before the inception of the round earth, all thoughts, concepts, were the product of the sensibility of life on a flat earth. The earth was flat until the point of creation of the round earth; which is not to say that the earth was flat until we realized that all along it had been round.

The information on the previous page is false. The previous page is the flat earth. This page is the round earth. The earth is round: this page is being read. If we talk of a flat earth producing a round earth: the round earth is doing the talking. If we talk of the previous page: this page is doing the talking. The previous page as an entity is the invention of this page, it can exist only on this page, it can live only on this page. We must not assume the existence of any entity until we are compelled to do so. Without this page the previous page could not have existence as an entity. The previous page exists as an entity only through decreation: this page decreates the previous page. Decreation of the thing described: assumption by this page of the description of the thing described: this page describing the previous page. Decreation: this page invents the previous page: round earth invents flat earth.

There is nothing more to invent, nothing more to play with. No creation, no becoming, no pretention, no intention: that's not how the show is run: / This independent mind, / Unkingdom'd, might as well be none. No one: Not the intense moment/ Isolated, with no before and after, / But a lifetime burning in every moment/ And not the lifetime of one man only/ But of old stones that cannot be deciphered.

And whatever you can do . . . there will be no difference.
And whatever you will do . . . there will be no difference.
And whatever you could do, don't do, should do . . . and whatever you do . . . there will be no difference.

Unitless unity: silence. But listen! When,/ If ever in the windings of the dance,/ To-be-said and saying in perfection fit,/ Another silence listens: listen again.

Stopping: never having started.

III

Disposable world.

The world is a waste system. A disposal of categories and names.

The world is no longer important. The world is no longer a thing: description is. It's a world of words. Words are finite: they signify nothing other than themselves. The word must be the thing it represents. Otherwise it is a symbol. It is a question of identity: there isn't any. There's no thinking subject: only words. Only descriptions.

No thinking subject. Metaphysical I, instead: not a part, but a limit. A unitless unity. The physical, the phenomenal world is gone. We are no longer a part of it. We never were a part of it. The world is finite: the objective world was no more real than the words that were its habit. A finite world of words: the world as limits of language. The limits of my language mean the limits of my world. No part, but limit. No longer any refuge in the infinities of grandeur, of the universe, of physicalized reality. No part, but limit. Never forget this finiteness, this limit of man.

Finite man: metaphysical I: unitless unity: no part, but limit. It means that there is no longer any possible distinction between observer and observed. It means that we live in a new whole, a new reality, one that is slippery, one that is expressed *in* language but cannot be expressed *by* language. It means that observing is completing and we are content in a world that shrinks to an immediate whole that we do not need to understand, complete without secret arrangements of it in the mind.

The same old fallacy persists—the desire to introduce a unity in the world: the mythologists made it a woman or an elephant; the scientists made fun of the mythologists, but themselves turned the world into the likeness of a mechanical toy. One analogy is as good as another.

The words of the world are the life of the world. It is the speech of truth in its true solitude: a nature that is created in what it says.

The world is no longer important: true. The world is the only important thing to think about: true. The world: a closed door. A closed door slammed in the face of man. It is a barrier. And at the same time it is the way through.

But through what? The physical world: an artifact, made or constructed of some basic, primary substance. The physical world is a created world: the production of something from nothing. The finite world, world of words: a new world, non-world: everything must come from everything. Description is the thing: the world is created in what it says. Created: thus destroyed. The physical world is meaningless: transfer physical to language.

Finite man: he disposes the world in categories. A waste system: there's no getting rid of them without naming them, that's the thing to keep in mind. Thus, any name, any definition or category empties the world as it creates it. It is a name that gives birth, gives life, while at the same time bringing separation and death. The world is a waste system of the unreal: nothing is left but the unreal. Just to name things.

The death of the world: the icy words hail down upon me, the icy meanings, and the world dies too . . . all I know is what the words know.

Tired of the old words, the comfort words, bored with the old descriptions. All categories are pseudo-categories. All categories, all concepts are waste. Magic, myth, religion, art . . . ideology, science, literature: comfort words. There is no longer any possibility of objective points of support outside speech or thought. Meaning and necessity are preserved only in the linguistic practices which embody them.

Thus, no meaning can be ascribed to "existing world." It is neither significant nor absurd. It *is*, quite simply. That is the most remarkable thing about it. And suddenly the obviousness of this strikes us with irresistible force. All at once the whole splendid construction collapses. And the world born of the word goes back to the word.

Universe is not a very large expanding balloon with galactic light bulbs interspersed at varying distances. $E=MC^2$ showed that Universe is not a simultaneous assembly of things. Universe isn't even *there*–in fact man's invention of the concept reveals his terror crouching behind a facade of omniscience. Universe: the most comprehensive world-generalization. Universe isn't *there:* it simply *is.* It's not a thing, or things: it *is.* It's not *how* things are in the world that is mystical, but *that* it exists.

We are deprived of our comfort words, our comfortable world. We are denied, everything is denied. Things no longer have any meaning. Things no longer exist. There is no longer the possibility of a universe of psychological, social, or functional signification. There is no longer the possibility of constructing a new objective world, even though it be more solid, more immediate. There is no longer the possibility of a single world, a whole world, a unified world.

The unity is unitless: man is dead. This is a terrifying concept for man to contemplate. Absolutely terrifying. We have tried to force reality into a framework of space and time just as the ancients tried to place reality within a framework of emotions. It doesn't work. Witness the image of the earth as seen from the moon: night and day at the same time: all times all the time: no matter what the time. Times have changed.

Everyone talks about the Earth being round but does anyone actually believe it? Nature of roundness is that you eventually get back to the same place—nowhere to go—no infinity. Not condensation, but condensation of mind. We are all living through one of our most terrifying dream horror fantasies: we're locked in a room, and the walls and ceilings are closing in on us. All the things we've been raised to worship—man's limitless power, the ever-giving nature of mother earth—all these infinite possibilities are beginning to seem less infinite. In fact, the infinite horizon is heading this way fast.

We can't even continue to talk of Earth: the place: a physical clump of dirt spinning around outer space: outside what. The world still goes spinning around, but it's in my head. It's happening in my head. I do it all in my head. It's a finite world of words: where is this world . . . and what do I know of it? Where do I seize it? Where do I believe it? Where do I surrender myself to it entirely? Here! Or nowhere.

Words do not signify anything but their own reality. Words do not create the universe out of nothing but out of all. All possibilities exist in any: the whole story from Genesis to Apocalypse in any event; in any metamorphoses. Therefore it is important to keep changing the subject. The subject changes before our very eyes.

What is: is something else. Finite man: he has no interest in what exists. He has no time for what is. No beginning, no ending. He lives without life: the story of life. It's over: never began. It's not a physical death, a physical end. It's simply that to tell a story has become strictly impossible. It's a world of words: saying is inventing . . . you invent nothing. Saying makes it so.

Beyond the world: a world of words with no beyond. No psychic walls of I's. No incommunicable mass of we's. A finite world of words: a sense of limit, a limit which does not energize subject matter, but penetrates it, dissolves it, creating both dream and reality, life and death. A finite world of words: you can't tell where the subject is, you can't tell what the subject is.

Reject the world. Metaphysical I instead: no part, but limit. Reject the world. Reject man. Be faithful to the conception of a limit. The new finite view of man: the rejection of humanism (doctrine that man is the measure): a complete anthropomorphization of the world, whether pantheism, idealism, or rationalism. Reject man. Reject the world. Reject the thinking subject for limit, the limit of language, a world created in what it says. I'm in words, made of words, other's words. . . . I'm all these words, all these strangers.

Man is no longer necessary. Neither are you. Man is dead: he is totally deprived. Of himself, even of nothing. There is nowhere to go in the absurdity of his lifetime. Any new style, any new life, any new world, is but a god where gods are no longer valid. The god that one so finds is but a word born of words, and returns to the word. For the reply we make to ourselves is assuredly never anything other than the question itself.

Reject world as unit. There is no phenomenal world as an external point of reference, of support. There is no possible communication between these illusory points. Communication is impossible: the thing said and the thing heard have a common source. And it's not an inventing mind, a thinking subject. Metaphysical I instead: no part, but limit. Me: I do it all in my head: what head?

A world full of sound and fury, signifying nothing. It points to nothing other than the fact that it is. It's not a metaphor. It's nothing you can believe in. It is. The moment you let it out of your head, it's dead: it's real.

Reject life in any number of "worlds" or "universes" or in trifling delusions such as "past," "present," or "future." It's all denied. Finite man in a finite world. Or, finite man as finite world.

The world is unintelligible. It is impossible to include it all under one large counter such as "God" or "Truth" and other verbalisms, or the disease of the symbolic language. All such words are comfort words. The world is unintelligible. There is no one way, no one. The world is unintelligible: the world is our intelligence. Here, now, we forget each other and ourselves. We feel the absurdity of an order, a whole, a knowledge, that which arranged the rendezvous, within its vital boundary, in the mind.

Any definition empties the world as it creates it. Empties it of all life. Any definition of the world fixes it. If it is fixed, it is dead. Only by a name do we know what is dead. Only through a category do we comprehend the unreal. Names and categories, names and definitions: comfort words. And nothing has been changed except what is unreal, as if nothing had been changed at all. Disposable world: comfort words: there's no getting rid of them without naming them and their contraptions, that's the thing to keep in mind.

In a world with no signification, in a world where psychic, social, and functional resolution is impossible, in a world where life lies hidden in language . . . the fate of the author is to have nothing, absolutely nothing to say. The book is a lie, the words have no author. To live in this world beyond the world, a world of words with no beyond, the author does not write about the world. Any attempt to do so is merely another fiction in a world of fictions. The aim of the book must be to attract subtlety, to attract complexity. But then, this is not a book, it has nothing to do with books, with literature. It can't be read: it's performance. Performance without a player. The author has no intention of its meaning.

All the notions by which we have lived are tottering. The sciences are calling the tune. Knowledge is now transitional. The real is no longer neatly delimited. Place, time, and matter admit of liberties that, not long ago, no one had an inkling of. Common sense is now appealed to only by the ignorant. The value of ordinary evidence is down to zero. What was once believed by all, always and everywhere, seems no longer to carry much weight. Knowledge is now transitional: it's something to forget.

When knowledge enters the room, forget it. None of the categories work, all explanations are wrong. Description vs. explanation: explanation is always wrong. It's a world of words, of descriptions, and description comes to an end, and we realize that it has left nothing behind it: it has instituted a double movement of creation and destruction.

Knowledge: the expression "to know everything" has as its complement the word universe. But to know everything includes knowing that the universe isn't even there. The universe is the big con. Our widest possible knowledge-world-generalization has dissolved into metaphysical ha-ha.

Universe is the big con. Physical theory is no longer "reality." We got lost once speculation was concerned no longer with subphenomena assumed to be similar to the phenomena directly observed, but rather with "things" that in no way resemble the things we know, since they only send us signals which we interpret as best we can. Plus our language, and our logic, our concepts have been found wanting: all this intellectual material will not fit into the nucleus of an atom, where everything is without precedent, without shape. Debatable probabilities have taken the place of definite and distinct facts and the fundamental distinction between observation and its object is no longer conceivable.

What in the world has happened? Simply that our means of investigation and action have far outstripped our means of representation and understanding. This is the enormous new fact that results from all the other new facts. This one is positively transcendent.

The squirming facts exceed the squamous mind. This new fact is positively transcendent. But in the new world, non-world of this new fact, there can be no transcendence. The world is finite: it can't fit into the terminology, into the constraints of humanistic consciousness. It will only be viewed there as an absence, as a negation of the terms and categories that inform Western man. It's not explainable. It won't be defined. It's bereft of all the dogma of rationalism, of humanism. Forget it.

No man is my friend. I have no interest in the human condition. No interest in you, your ideas, your words. No interest in your opinions.

Don't believe it. Don't believe anything I say. There's nothing to say. I have nothing to say. There's nothing to think about.

Disposable world: enigmatic world. Epistemological enigma: the facts of inquiry dissolve into the reality of the enquirer, casting further doubt on both. The world is a waste system of extinct epistemologies.

One is the great signifier: creator of all the comfort words: God, Truth, Humanity, Writer, etc. One is obsolete. We can no longer deal with single level definitions. It doesn't follow that there are multiple level definitions either. There is no signification. One doesn't signify. One obscures. There is no identity beyond the words that are its representation. There is no identity: words are what count. One musn't let one get in the way.

There can be no psychic, social, or functional resolution of all this. We must get back to the source. But there is no source. The source, the one reality is not to be found. There is no source. There is no answer.

I beseech you enter your life. I beseech you learn to say "I," when I question you: For you are no part, but a whole. No portion, but a being.

A leap over the psychic walls of man. Drop the body: the physicalized conception of perception. Meditate the putrifying corpse. The discovery of the private individual form: thank God for the names of the body.

Crashing through the personal psychic walls. I am out of my mind. The lives lived in the mind are at an end. They never were. Were and are not. It is not to be believed. I am out of my mind. Out of the personal psyche. He was not a man yet he was nothing else. If in the mind, he vanished, taking there the mind's own limits, like a tragic thing. Without existence, existing everywhere.

Self-conscious option isn't enough: self-conscious option is too much. There's no thinking subject. Thus, it's not a question of thinking. It's not a question of thinking but of that which is its intelligence. It's of intelligence that I must think.

Description once claimed to reproduce a pre-existing reality; it now asserts its creative function. It once made us see things, now it seems to destroy them, as if its intention to discuss them aimed only at blurring their contours, at making them incomprehensible, at causing them to disappear altogether. Man is dead: but the humanist, the modern man instructed by the terms of liberal thought and conventions, will be completely unable to understand this uncompromising attitude of finiteness.

The world is made up, not made. The world is created, and created things can no longer be considered as intermediaries leading to an infinity of other things. They are dead: they are their own fictions, begin and end in themselves, live and die in themselves. Created things are dead. The life you live is a lie. The world you inhabit is a lie. There is no need for fiction in the world: the world is the only fiction.

Personality is not the only way. The individual is one of the problems of our time. So, too, the mass of men. What to do about amount, what to do about quantity. They're nothing, starting from one. In a finite world, numbers don't count: words do. There's no addition, no accretion, no infinite attainments. Nothing and everything, no one and everyone: man is dead. The mass is nothing. The number of men in a mass of men is nothing. The mass is no greater than the singular man of the mass.

Finite man, finite intelligence: control. Not in control, but as control, as reality, as intelligence. Finite intelligence: the mass is no greater than the singular man of the mass. Expect no life from the mass. Expect no voice from the people.

Life is inexpressible. Life is inexcusable.

It's getting much harder to live. It's getting much easier to accept the idea that it is an illusion that we were ever alive. Life is a knowledge, not an existence. Life is disposing of the waste: names and categories. Name it: it's dead. Then you live in those names and by those names. You live in those names and by those names when you live in the world.

It's no longer possible to tell a story: life is a story. It's a story, a narrative series of pictures. A series of timeless tableaus, an infinitely successive series of nows. But this can't be. It isn't. A picture held us captive. And we could not get outside it, for it lay in our language and language seemed to repeat it to us inexorably. The world is finite: that means "it" isn't. We are free from the pictures and the lives lived in the mind are at an end. Words are what matter.

I'm going out of my mind. I'm trying to hold on to my body, my life. It's a horrifying experience.

We had thought to control it by assigning it a meaning, but the world has only, little by little, lost all its life. Man is dead. It's not enough to perish. One has to become unintelligible, almost ridiculous.

No sign of life but life, itself, the presence of the intelligible in that which is created as its symbol. Life is a knowledge, not an existence. Life is not lived, it is known. Known: not experienced. Imagine, you had an experience.

Disposable world. A reality of decreation: to make something created pass into the uncreated. Modern reality is a reality of decreation, in which our revelations are not the revelations of belief, but the precious portents of our own powers.

To make something created pass into the uncreated: no action, but realization. All created things are dead things. They belong to the world. We participate in the creation of the world by decreating ourselves, by peopling the world with the dead images of mankind.

The created world is a world of waste, of life. And life is the elimination of what is dead. We give names to things that can't be named: we create life, we create death. Creation: the waste system. Life is the elimination of what is dead.

All these things. All these people. All these places. All this waste, this garbage: it's me. There was never anyone, anyone but me, anything but me, talking to me of me. When I dream and invent without a backward glance, am I not . . . Nature?

Dispense with the notion of nature: a creative power that makes something from nothing. Nature is scenery built up by man. Man is dead. The unity is unitless. There is no continuity, no accretion, no incremental serial advances, no depth. There is no nature. There was never anyone but me talking to me of me. No nature: just a nature created in what it says.

Dismiss yourself. Man is dead. There's no nature but a fall, into the state of nature. The spirit, the human essence, hides, buried in the natural object: "projected" . . . the death of gods and the birth of poetry. A nature created in what it says.

Each herb and each tree, mountain, hill, earth and sea, cloud, meteor and star, are men seen afar. There are no external points of support in reality. The unity is unitless: this is not just a rival to an objective reality. There is no real world: it is an illusion. The unity is unitless. This is the whole truth, and it can only be apprehended through its contrast with the illusion, the real world. Thus, man perceives in the world only what already lies within him; but to perceive what lies within him, man needs the world.

Take the real out of the world and put it back where it belongs, where it always has been: realization. Any system that attempts to base a pattern of thought, or a linguistic practice, on some independent foundation in reality, is impossible. Any system is impossible. If these systems need any justification, it must lie within them, because there are no independent points of support outside them. That kind of objectivism is an illusion, produced, no doubt, by the reassuring character of explanation, which is that any support that is needed comes from the center, man himself.

But the center has dissolved. Man is dead: the great explainer, the great explanation. He has lost the center: he was the center, the whole in which he was contained. There can be no more explanations, no more worlds.

There is no center, no source. You can't explain what isn't there. Metaphysical I, nonphysical I: it's the fault of pronouns, there is no name for me, no pronoun for me, all the trouble comes from that.

No center, no source, no whole, no one: and now no me. What in the world do you do? It's a lot to expect of one creature that he should first behave as if he were not, then as if he were, before being admitted to that peace where he neither is, nor is not, and where the language dies that permits of such expressions.

The physical world is no longer real. That rational, reasoned, objective world of classical science and humanistic thought is now positively mystical and occult. Combat all rationalist dogmas that stand in the way of a metaphysical universe. Man is dead. Metaphysical I instead. Not reality, but realization. Dismiss yourself. Let go: there's nothing lost.

This is the age of unimportance. Reject world. Reject external reality: reject internal reality. Say no to yourself, to your great truths, to your great men, to your great books.

Not revelations of belief, not the Capital Letters: Truth, God, Freedom, Justice, Will . . . but the precious portents of our own powers: the limits of my language mean the limits of my world. Finite man: he made a personal matter of what had before his time been treated in dogmatic form, dominated by tradition. He had no use for anything except evidence or observation scrupulously verified. What this amounted to was a refusal to attach to language any value derived merely from people or books . . . his self tipped the balance.

No more great men, no more great books: his self tipped the balance. His realization was the balance: is the balance. But in a finite world, even the self is denied, reduced to an object. No more great men, no more great books . . . no more importance. Deny your own validity. . . . Surrender to the flux, to the drift towards a new and unthinkable order. Uproot yourself. Uproot yourself, socially and vegetatively. Exile yourself from every earthly country.

No: negation is the only way, there is no way. The universe must be created out of all, not created from nothing. Created by negation for creating or not creating changes nothing. Changes nothing because all created things are unreal: are nothing. Negation is the only way: no.

Finite man: he says no to everything in order to get at himself. Yet he's not alive, he's not himself. He lives in his image: the unreal.

What is: is other things. Man is dead. He lives in his image: the unreal. How can anyone be what one is? No sooner does the question occur to us than it takes us out of ourselves, and at once we see how impossible we are. Immediately we are astonished at being someone, at the absurdity of every individual fact of existence, at the curious effect of seeing our acts, beliefs and persons duplicated; everything human is too human—an oddity, a delusion, a reflex, a nonsense. The system of conventions becomes comic, sinister, unbearable to think of, almost unbelievable! Laws, religion, customs, clothes, beliefs . . . all seem curiosities, a masquerade.

Metaphysical I: of whom I know nothing. I don't know who I am. There is no signifiable reality. No one truth, no essence. It's slippery: there's nothing left to hold on to. We are completely deprived. You are totally denied. And I: I don't know who I am. It has not yet been our good fortune to establish with any degree of accuracy what I am, where I am, whether I am words among words, or silence in the midst of silence.

I: words among words or silence in the midst of silence. The final answer will be in the transcendence of all categories, of all names: the death of the word. But this can't be so: there is no transcendence: no answer. World is finite: there is no distinction between observation and its object. Not reality, but realization. Transcendence belongs to the real, infinite world: reality. But there can be no transcendence of realization: no distinction between observation and its object. No differentiation: there was never anyone but me talking to me of me. And me: I go where the words go: nowhere. There is no final perfection, no answer. No one.

Our kind of innovation consists not in the answers, but in the true novelty of the questions themselves; in the statement of problems, not in their solutions. What is important is not to illustrate a truth—or even an interrogation—known in advance, but to bring to the world certain interrogations . . . not yet known as such to themselves.

A total synthesis of all human knowledge will not result in fantastic amounts of data, or in huge libraries filled with books. There's no value any more in amount, in quantity, in explanation. For a total synthesis of human knowledge, use the interrogative. Ask the most subtle sensibilities in the world what questions they are asking themselves.

The words have no author. There are words better without an author, without a poet, or having a separate author, a different poet, an accretion from ourselves, intelligent, beyond intelligence, an artificial man. The words have no author. The book is a lie. It's a performance: by a reader. Reader is a comfort word and the author has no intention of its meaning. Author is a comfort word and the author has no intention of its meaning.

An accretion from ourselves, intelligent, by an intelligence, an artificial man. Unreal realization: freedom is like a man who kills himself each night, an incessant butcher. Artificial man: he's not himself: unreal realization. He is revealed, secularized as a thing, an object. He has lost the whole in which he was contained. He has shed his human clothes.

Just as the ancients peopled the universe, we have set out to empty it of all life. It's a finite world of words: there is no life in man, there is no existence in things, there is no evolution in nature. Man is dead: drowned in the depth of things (of himself), man ultimately no longer even perceives them: his role is soon limited to experiencing, in their name, totally humanized impressions and desires. But there is no depth in things. Words are what count: the word must be the thing it represents. Words are finite: there can be no depth, no interiority.

There's no perfection in humanity. Man was considered the perfect center in a world of infinite things, infinite depth. But man has been rooted out of his human home, disallowed his humanistic habit. Man is dead: he is "thinged," he is artificial: he mocks his own meaning, he's not to be believed.

But humanism attempts to recover *everything*, including whatever attempts to retrace its limits, even to impugn it as a whole. No matter what: there is man and his nature. And a common nature must be the eternal answer to the single question of our civilization—only one possible answer to everything: man.

This humanistic attitude is considered the inevitable attitude of the emancipated and instructed man. But answers are no answer: there's no perfection in humanity. Man is an extraordinarily fixed and limited animal, whose nature is absolutely constant. A veritable object. Man is a sick animal: to think he can be cured is to imprison him in the disease.

What was an animal? It is the human that is alien, the human that has a cousin on the moon, the human that demands speech from beasts and the incommunicable mass.

The mass. The human mass. The impossible agglomerate mass. The incommunicable human mass. The people. From their places masses move, stark as laws. Masses of what? One does not ask. There somewhere man is too, vast conglomerate of all of nature's kingdoms, as lonely and as bound. The impossible people.

The mass is nothing: the people aren't. It's the human that is alien. Man is dead: the men have no shadows. A man is a result, a demonstration. An unreal realization.

I am out of my mind. Beyond the I to something else. A place of nothing else and no beyond. I am out of my mind. Deprived even of my I. The I which becomes merely a more immediate object in the wasteland of objects. And the role of objects is to restore silence, for objects are no more real than the words that are their habit. I am out of my mind: am I words in the midst of words or silence in the midst of silence.

The narrator is gone. The universe as a narrative story isn't there. Evolution as a narrative story never happened: words are what matter. Evolution is a matter of the words used to describe it. There is no continuous, infinite, evolving world-universe-nature-knowledge waiting to be explained by man. It's a word of words: a nature created in what it says.

The universe isn't there. Man is dead. But I can find no way of escape from what is not! Speech so fills us, fills everything with its images that we cannot think how to begin to refrain from imagining–nothing is without it. . . . Remember that tomorrow is a myth, that the universe is one; that numbers, love, the real and the infinite . . . that justice, the people, poetry . . . the earth itself are myths. The universe isn't there. It is.

Don't believe any of this. Place no value in the book, in the author. Private authorship or ownership is not to be respected. It is all one book. Give it up, the idea of an author, of truth. Give up all belief: believe only in yourself. You: your experience is my experience. Me: it's of me now that I must speak, even if I have to do it with their language. Them: I slip into them. . . . it is a stratum, strata, without debris or vestiges. But it's a world filled with debris and vestiges: before I am done I shall find traces of what was. What was: is me, never anyone but me talking to me of me, in words, made of words, other's words, what others . . . the whole world is here with me. Me: I don't. I don't believe any of this.

I can't think of one anymore. This or that: I can't differentiate anymore. I don't believe it: I can't think, I must not try to think, simply utter. Saying makes it so. This, this and that: I shall have to banish them in the end, the beings, shapes, sounds, and lights with which my haste to speak has encumbered this place.

The necessity of stopping before starting. The necessity to forget it all.

Nobody knows, and you can't find out.

NOTES: I

Bracketed figures in italic type refer to pages in this book.

[*9*] Norbert Wiener, *I Am a Mathematician* (Cambridge, Mass.: M.I.T. Press, 1956), p. 323. "The world about . . . system can transmit."

[*10*] Karl S. Lashley, "Cerebral Organization and Human Behavior," in Harry G. Solomon *et al.* (eds.), *The Brain and Human Behavior* (New York: Hafner Publishing Co., Inc., 1966), p. 4. "there are order . . . considered the organizer."

[*11*] George Kubler, *The Shape of Time* (New Haven, Conn.: Yale University Press, 1967), p. 17. "The rest of . . . being are projected."

[*15*] J. Z. Young, *Doubt and Certainty in Science* (London: Oxford University Press, 1962), p. 16. "Any system . . . it's own stability."

[*16*] John C. Lilly, *The Mind of a Dolphin* (New York: Doubleday & Company, Inc., 1967), p. 103. "Information does not . . . of these data."

[*17*] (1) Young, op. cit., p. 17. "To speak of . . . to the change."
(2) Lilly, op. cit., p. 104. "The mind of . . . bits of signals."

[*18*] (1) H. Marshall McLuhan, *Understanding Media: The Extensions of Man* (New York: McGraw-Hill Book Company, 1964), p. 26. "Effect involves the . . . of information movement."
(2) Stuart Brand, correspondence. "All that's traceably . . . except through effects."

[*19*] (1) Heinz von Foerster, "Logical Structure of Environment and Its Internal Representation," in R. E. Eckerstrom (ed.), *International Design Conference, Aspen, 1962* (Zeeland, Mich.: Herman Miller, Inc., 1963). "program is nothing . . . don't do that . . . ."
(2) Lilly, op. cit., p. 104. "a brain and . . . body, another brain."

[*21*] Edward T. Hall, conversation. Professor Hall pointed out to the author that "we're talking." Theme is developed in Professor Hall's books: *The Hidden Dimension* (New York: Doubleday & Company, Inc., 1966) and *The Silent Language* (New York: Doubleday & Company, Inc., 1959).

[*22*] Wiener, op. cit., p. 325. "new concepts of . . . and of society."

[*23*] Alfred North Whitehead, *Science and the Modern World* (New York: The Free Press, 1967), p. 59. "it is of . . . period of progress."

[*26*] W. Grey Walter, *The Living Brain* (New York: W. W. Norton & Company, Inc., 1963), p. 148. "The supreme abstraction . . . glimpses of itself."

[*27*] Kenneth M. Sayre, "Philosophy and Cybernetics," in Frederick J. Crosson and Kenneth M. Sayre (eds.), *Philosophy and Cybernetics* (New York: Simon and Schuster, Inc., 1967), p. 20. "Neither the presence . . . his observable behavior."

[*28*] René Descartes. "*Cogito ergo sum.*"

[*29*] (1) Benjamin Lee Whorf, *Language, Thought, and Reality* (Cambridge, Mass.: M.I.T. Press, 1956), p. 252. "an unfortunate word . . . characterized by patterning."
(2) Niels Bohr, *Atomic Physics and Human Knowledge* (New York: Science Editions, Inc., 1961), p. 76. "Only by renouncing . . . account its characteristics."

[*30*] (1) Ibid., p. 91. "the description of . . . simple physical pictures."
(2) Ibid., p. 70. "represent relations for . . . for objective description."

[*31*] Von Foerster, op. cit. "A measure of . . . b with a."

[*33*] (1) Bohr, op. cit., pp. 78–79. "In return for . . . object-subject separation."
(2) Von Foerster, op. cit. "not only a . . . observing this universe."

[*34*] René Dubos, *Man, Medicine, and Environment* (New York: Frederick A. Praeger, Inc., 1968), p. 118. "The past experience . . . their ultimate expressions."

[*38*] (1) D. and K. Stanley-Jones, *The Kybernetics of Living Systems* (New York: Pergamon Press, Inc., 1960), p. 55. The only unit . . . or permeability-wave.
(2) Ibid., p. 53. "each local area . . . source of origin."
(3) Ibid. "It matters nothing . . . of the telegraph."

[*39*] (1) Ibid. "The qualities of . . . or frequency varies."

(2) Ibid. "namely, the diameter . . . of the procession."
(3) Ibid. "It is these . . . may be constructed."

[*40*] Ibid., pp. 53–54. "If an operation . . . bell was rung."

[*41*] Ibid., p. 54. "The mechanism whereby . . . the single track."

[*45*] John Lucas, "Minds, Machines, and Godel," in Kenneth M. Sayre and Frederick J. Crosson (eds.), *The Modeling of Mind Computers and Intelligence* (New York: Simon and Schuster, Inc., 1968), p. 255. for any formal system . . . within the system.

[*49*] Norbert Wiener, *Cybernetics* (Cambridge, Mass.: M.I.T. Press, 1967), p. 199. "It is important . . . the imposed disturbance."

[*50*] Carlos Castenedas, *The Teachings of Don Juan* (Berkeley, Calif.: University of California Press, 1968), p. 76. "All paths are . . . they lead nowhere."

[*51*] (1) *New York Post,* April 17, 1968, p. 11. Deaths were caused . . . faulty television tubes.
(2) *Popular Science,* February, 1968, p. 79. Scientific institutes warned . . . could cause cancer.

[*52*] (1) Walter, op. cit., p. 68. The most obvious . . . for the brain,
(2) René Dubos, *Man Adapting* (New Haven, Conn.: Yale University Press, 1967), pp. 49–51. "in all animal . . . the human species."

[*53*] Ibid., p. 54. "there may well . . . environmental periodicities."

[*57*] (1) Norbert Wiener, *Extrapolation, Interpolation, and Smoothing of Stationary Time Series* (Cambridge, Mass.: M.I.T. Press, 1949), p. 2. "A message need . . . transmission of ideas."
(2) Ibid., p. 3. "The main function . . . it's own technique."

[*58*] Walter, op. cit., p. 189. "the parts of . . . stimulation has ceased."

[*60*] (1) Stanley-Jones, op. cit., p. 60. The visual receptors . . . of neural energy.
(2) Wiener, *Cybernetics,* pp. 134–35. "The human eye . . . range as possible."

[*63*] (1) Dubos, *Man, Medicine, and Environment,* p. 40. "Mechanisms for perceiving . . . by earlier stimulation."
(2) Ibid., p. 41. The information received . . . of new programs.
(3) Ibid. "The ability to . . . the early ones."

(4) Wiener, *Cybernetics,* p. 124. There is reason . . . the storage elements.

[*64*] (1) Stanley-Jones, op. cit., pp. 19–21. The orthosympathetic systems . . . through the system.

(2) Dubos, *Man Adapting,* p. 29. The hormonal changes . . . performance actually begins.

[*65*] Vishvassara Tantra. "what's here's everywhere; what's not here's nowhere."

[*66*] Edward T. Hall, *The Hidden Dimension* (New York: Doubleday & Company, Inc., 1966), p. 4. Man created his . . . use of it.

[*72*] Sören Kierkegaard, quoted in Loren Eiseley, *The Firmament of Time* (New York: Atheneum Publishers, 1966), p. 117. "The future is not."

[*75*] Lashley, in Solomon *et al.,* p. 2. "a man thinks . . . good to eat."

[*78*] (1) Wilder Penfield, "Functional Localization in Temporal and Deep Sylvan Areas," in Solomon *et al.,* p. 219. Electrical stimulation of . . . different from real.

(2) R. G. Bickford, D. W. Mulder, H. W. Dodge, Jr., H. J. Svien, and H. P. Rome, "Changes in Memory Function Produced by Electrical Stimulation of the Temporal Lobe in Man," in Solomon *et al.,* p. 232. "By appropriate electrical . . . the phenomenon elicited."

[*81*] Young, op. cit., p. 16. The key to . . . of man's communication.

[*83*] Wiener, *The Human Use of Human Beings,* p. 132. Where man went, so went man's information.

[*92*] (1) Penfield, in Solomon *et al.,* p. 219. Illusions of familiarity . . . for minor-handedness.

(2) Walter, op. cit., pp. 98–100. the flicker experience . . . exaggerated electrical discharge.

[*95*] Young, op. cit., p. 19. "a sense in . . . and his products."

[*96*] Whorf, op. cit., p. 239. "it may even . . . now call 'mental.'"

[*97*] Werner Heisenberg, *Philosophic Problems of Nuclear Science* (New York: Fawcett World Library, 1966), p. 106. "When we talk . . . by their application."

NOTES: II

[*106*] (1) Sir James Jeans, *The Mysterious Universe* (New York: E. P. Dutton & Co., 1932), pp. 117–18. "*Entia non sunt* . . . takes something away."

(2) Ludwig Wittgenstein, *Zettel*, eds. G. E. M. Anscombe and G. H. von Wright, trans. G. E. M. Anscombe (Berkeley: University of California Press, 1967), p. 73e, para. 410. "A person can . . . learned to calculate."

(3) Alfred North Whitehead, *Process and Reality* (New York: Harper & Row, Publishers, 1960), p. 14. "Progress is always . . . what is obvious."

(4) Wallace Stevens, "Adagia," is *Opus Posthumous* (New York: Alfred A. Knopf, 1966), p. 157. "progress in any . . . changes of terminology."

[*107*] (1) Leon Brillouin, *Scientific Uncertainty and Information* (New York: Academic Press, Inc., 1964), p. 64. "A no man's . . . past and future."

(2) Wittgenstein, op. cit., p. 116e, paras. 662–64. "a seeing into . . . past to us."

[*109*] Ludwig Wittgenstein, *Tractatus Logico-Philosophicus*, trans. D. F. Pears and B. F. McGuiness (New York: The Humanities Press, 1960), p. 13, para. 5.4732. "point is that . . . language mean nothing."

[*111*] T. S. Eliot, "Choruses from 'The Rock,'" in *The Complete Poems and Plays, 1909–1950* (New York: Harcourt, Brace & World, 1962), p. 107. "a moment in . . . gave the meaning."

[*112*] Whitehead, *Process and Reality*, p. 13. "the primary advantage . . . of common sense."

[*113*] I. A. Richards, "Complementary Complementarities," in *The Screens and Other Poems* (New York: Harcourt, Brace & World, 1960), p. 34. "Where you end . . . draw a line."

[*114*] (1) Gertrude Stein, *Lectures in America* (Boston: Beacon Press, 1935), pp. 209–10. "A noun is . . . write about it."

(2) Eliot, "Four Quartets," op. cit., p. 126. "the growing terror . . . to think about."

[*115*] Wallace Stevens, "The Latest Freed Man," in *The Collected Poems of Wallace Stevens* (New York: Alfred A. Knopf, 1967), p. 205. "To be without description of to be."

[*116*] Stevens, "Notes Toward a Supreme Fiction," Ibid., p. 389. "The final elegance . . . plainly to propound."

[*117*] (1) Stevens, "The Sail of Ulysses," in *Opus Posthumous*, p. 102. "Of gods and . . . which they symbolized."

(2) Jeans, op. cit., p. 49. "All the pictures . . . are mathematical pictures."

[*118*] (1) Niels Bohr, op. cit., p. 68. "a refinement of . . . imprecise or cumbersome."

(2) Ibid. "Just by avoiding . . . for objective description."

[*119*] Stevens. "The Man with the Blue Guitar," in *Collected Poems*, p. 183. "Throw away the . . . the rotted names."

[*120*] (1) Jeans, op. cit., p. 173. "We need no . . . of the moment."
(2) Ibid., p. 174. "exists in a . . . the ultimate reality."

[*121*] (1) Niels Bohr, "Dialectica I," 318, quoted in Richards, "Complementary Complementarities," p. 36. "Our task can . . . its strict definition."
(2) Whitehead, op. cit., p. 19. "There are no . . . ill-defined and ambiguous."

[*122*] Brillouin, op. cit., p. 52. "The model need . . . we observe it."

[*123*] (1) Max Born, *Experiment and Theory in Physics* (New York: Dover Publications, Inc., 1956), p. 39. "A physical quantity . . . and measure it."
(2) Jeans, op. cit., p. 172. "The making of . . . away from reality."
(3) Stevens, "Adagia," p. 168. "the word must be the thing it represents."

[*124*] (1) Whitehead, op. cit., p. 43. "the notion of . . . is completely abandoned."
(2) Ibid. "An actual entity . . . lost sight of."
(3) Wallace Stevens, *The Necessary Angel* (New York: Random House, Inc., 1951), p. 122. "The poet and his subject are inseparable."
(4) Richards, "Spring," op. cit., p. 21. "Before the birth . . . Are both undone!"

[*125*] (1) J. Andrade e Silva and G. Lochak, *Quanta* (New York: McGraw-Hill, 1969), p. 150. "To measure is to disturb."
(2) Brillouin, op. cit., p. 43. "We used to . . . stopped observing it."
(3) Whitehead, op. cit., p. 7. "we can never catch the world taking a holiday."
(4) Ibid. "the method of . . . observation, breaks down."
(5) Sir James Jeans, *The New Background of Science* (Ann Arbor: University of Michigan Press, 1959), p. 2. "Each observation destroys . . . become past history."
(6) Brillouin, op. cit., p. 52. "We cannot abstract . . . a mixed crowd." "absolutely renounce . . . objective real world."
(7) Jeans, op. cit., p. 287. "our observation of nature, and not nature itself."

[*126*] (1) Brillouin, op. cit., p. 50. "Experiments are the only elements which really count."
(2) Werner Heisenberg, *Physics and Philosophy* (New York: Harper & Row, 1958), p. 186. "The elementary particles . . . things and facts."

(3) Andrade e Silva and Lochak, op. cit., p. 148 (quoting Goethe). "Do not look . . . up the doctrine."

(4) Stevens, *Necessary Angel*, p. 95. "To confront fact . . . of the thing."

[*127*] Stevens, "Life on a Battleship," in *Opus Posthumous*, p. 79. "We approach a society/ Without a society."

[*128*] Stevens, "Notes Toward a Supreme Fiction," op. cit., p. 383. "The first idea was not our own."

[*129*] Wittgenstein, *Zettel*, p. 58e, para. 315. "Why do you . . . are at present."

[*131*] (1) Ibid., p. 199e, para. 687. "Why is a . . . than a tautology."

(2) Stein, op. cit., p. 11. "Knowledge is the . . . you do know."

[*134*] (1) Max Born, quoted in Brillouin, op. cit., p. 36. "Concepts which refer . . . of physical continuity."

(2) Ibid., p. 35. "An infinitely small . . . space and time."

(3) Jeans, op. cit., p. 294. "events must be . . . fundamental objective constituents."

(4) P. W. Bridgman, *The Way Things Are* (New York: Viking Press, 1959), p. 3. "analysis in terms of doings or happenings.

(5) Jeans, *Mysterious Universe*, p. 118. "Nature is such . . . any experiment whatsoever."

[*135*] (1) Wittgenstein, *Logico-Philosophicus*, p. 143, para. 6.362. "What can be described can also happen."

(2) Stevens, "The Man on the Dump," in *Collected Poems*, p. 203. "Where was it one first heard of the truth? The the."

[*136*] (1) Eliot, "Four Quartets," op. cit., p. 132. "The past has . . . Or even development."

(2) Bohr, op. cit., p. 7. "No pictorial interpretation . . . relations between observations."

[*137*] R. Buckminster Fuller, *Operating Manual for Spaceship Earth* (Carbondale: Southern Illinois University Press, 1969), p. 65. "One picture of . . . the butterfly stage."

[*139*] Andrade e Silva and Lochak, op. cit., p. 157. "to know is to measure."

[*140*] Eliot, "The Love Song of J. Alfred Prufrock," op. cit., p. 7. "Do I dare to eat a peach?"

[*142*] Eliot, "Four Quartets," op. cit., p. 139. "If you came . . . or carry report."

[*143*] (1) Sir Arthur Eddington, *The Philosophy of Physical Science* (Ann Arbor: University of Michigan Press, 1958),

p. 31. "Physical knowledge is . . . actual or hypothetical."
(2) Brillouin, op. cit., p. 10. "The study of . . . that of scarcity."
(3) William Empson, "Value Is in Activity," in *Collected Poems* (New York: Harcourt, Brace & Co., 1949), p. 4. "Value is in activity."
(4) Brillouin, op. cit., p. 100. "Only the final sum matters."
(5) Eddington, op. cit., p. 142. "Physical science consists . . . impenetrable mathematical symbol."

[*145*] (1) Wittgenstein, *Zettel*, pp. 12–13e, paras. 57–58. "finding to show . . . in our language."
(2) C. G. Jung, *VII Sermones Ad Mortuous* (London: Stuart & Watkins) "that hallowed and . . . the same time."
(3) Stevens, "Notes Toward a Supreme Fiction," op. cit., p. 387. "a form to . . . in the word."

[*147*] Stevens, "The Man on the Dump," op. cit., p. 203. "Is it peace . . . On the dump."

[*150*] Wittgenstein, op. cit., p. 17e, para. 88. "It is very . . . never interests us."

[*151*] Ibid., p. 35e, para. 198. "Can I think . . . it does not?"

[*152*] Whitehead, *Process and Reality*, p. 44. "The actual occasions are . . . ground of obligation."

[*153*] Ibid. "express the definiteness . . . ingression is realized."

[*154*] Brillouin, op. cit., p. 49. "Any absolute statement . . . can be valid."

[*155*] (1) Eliot, "Four Quartets," op. cit., p. 145. "costing not less than everything."
(2) Eliot, "The Love Song of J. Alfred Prufrock," Ibid., pp. 4–5. "Do I dare/ Disturb the universe?"
(3) Stevens, "Solitaire Under the Oaks," in *Opus Posthumous*, p. 111. "In the oblivion . . . trees, completely released."

[*156*] Stevens, "Life on a Battleship," op. cit., p. 79. "The part/ Is the equal of the whole."

[*159*] (1) Whitehead, op. cit., p. 53. "There is a . . . from common sense."
(2) Ibid. "There is a . . . continuity of becoming."
(3) Eliot, "Four Quartets," op. cit., p. 138. "This is the . . . in time's covenant." "Where is the . . . Zero summer."

[*160*] Stein, op. cit., p. 169. "No matter how . . . was no repetition."

[*161*] Empson, "This Last Pain," op. cit., p. 33. "Feign then what's . . . from a despair."

[*162*] Fuller, op. cit., pp. 62–63. "Physical experiments have . . . metaphysical, is finite."

[*163*] (1) Empson, "Doctrinal Point," op. cit., p. 39. "All physics one . . . of the description."
(2) Eddington, op. cit., p. 32. "Progress so far . . . unobserved and unobservable."

[*164*] Jeans, *Mysterious Universe,* p. 176. "Most men find . . . an imperishable universe."

[*165*] (1) Whitehead, op. cit., p. 17. "Every proposition proposing . . . for the fact."
(2) Wittgenstein, *Zettel,* pp. 120–21e, para. 695. "Understanding a commission . . . got to do."

[*166*] (1) Jeans, op. cit., p. 172. "The final truth . . . is at fault."
(2) Stevens, "Description Without Place," in *Collected Poems,* p. 344. "Description is revelation . . . nor false facsimile."

[*167*] (1) Eliot, "Four Quartets," op. cit., p. 144. "Every phrase and . . . to the block."
(2) Ibid. p. 126. "hope would be hope for the wrong thing." "love would be love of the wrong thing."

[*170*] Stevens, "Adagia," *Opus,* p. 164. "The exquisite environment . . . not realized before."

[*172*] (1) Eliot, "Four Quartets," op. cit., p. 122. "Ridiculous the waste . . . before and after."
(2) I. A. Richards, "The Status of the Mentionable," in *Goodbye Earth and Other Poems* (New York: Harcourt, Brace & Co., 1958), p. 29. "Hill, cloud, field . . . And must."

[*173*] Stein, op. cit., p. 172. "Anybody can be . . . at all important."

[*174*] (1) Richards, "To Dumb Forgetfulness," op. cit., p. 52. "Forget, forget . . . dead be dead."
(2) Richards, "The Status of the Mentionable," op. cit., p. 29. "Will, doubt, desire . . . To naught."
(3) Richards, "To Be," op. cit., p. 25. "still missing it . . . what, none know."

[*175*] (1) Wittgenstein, *Logico-Philosophicus,* p. 113, para 5.556. "There cannot be . . . we ourselves construct."
(2) Ludwig Wittgenstein, *Notebooks, 1914–16* (New York: Harper & Row, 1969), p. 52, para. 27.5.15. "what cannot be expressed we do not express."

[*176*] (1) Whitehead, op. cit., p. 44. "A multiplicity merely . . . its individual members."

(2) Stevens, "The Man with the Blue Guitar," *Collected Poems*, p. 171. "It is the chord that falsifies."
(3) Stevens, "Thirteen Ways of Looking at a Blackbird," op. cit., p. 92. "A man and . . . blackbird/ Are one."

[*177*] (1) Bertrand Russell, quoted in Jeans, *The New Background of Science*, p. 295. "Not a persistent . . . than fleeting thoughts."
(2) Jeans, Ibid. "Matter of solid . . . of human spectacles."

[*178*] Whitehead, op. cit., p. 20. "No language can . . . to immediate experience."

[*179*] Empson, "Doctrinal Point," op. cit., p. 39. "the duality of . . . unconsciousness of foreknowledge."

[*180*] Richards, "The Ruins," op. cit., p. 44. "So which way's . . . All idle theory."

[*182*] (1) William Butler Yeats, "The Second Coming," in *The Collected Poems of W. B. Yeats* (New York: The Macmillan Company, 1960), p. 184. "Things fall apart."
(2) Empson, "Letter V," op. cit., p. 41. "You are a metaphor and they are lies."
(3) Richards, "Not No," op. cit., p. 21. "Not mine this life that must be lived in me."
(4) Wittgenstein, *Zettel*, p. 40e, para. 220. "Do you look . . . your own breast."
(5) Stevens, "The Man on the Dump," op. cit., pp. 202–3. "One beats and . . . Be merely oneself?"

[*183*] (1) Eliot, "Four Quartets," op. cit., p. 114. "A people without . . . Of timeless moments."
(2) John McHale, correspondence. See McHale, John, *The Future of the Future* (New York: George Braziller, 1969). "Ahistory: Amen."

[*184*] (1) Eliot, "Four Quartets," op. cit., p. 117. "All time is eternally present."
(2) Ibid., p. 129. "Here and there . . . a deeper communion."

[*185*] Stein, op. cit., p. 195. "The composition we . . . thing to know."

[*186*] Stevens, "Description Without Place," op. cit., p. 345. "The theory of . . . of the world."

[*188*] Eliot, "Four Quartets," op. cit., p. 133. "We had the . . . beyond any meaning."

[*190*] Ibid., p. 125. "only a limited . . . we have been."

[*191*] (1) Richards, "The Screens," in *The Screens and other Poems*, p. 26. "An instrument which . . . it as well."

(2) Stevens, "Men Made Out of Words," op. cit., p. 355. "Life consists/ Of propositions about life."
(3) Rudolph Wurlitzer, *Nog* (New York: Random House, 1968), p. 84. "It's the next . . . from a name."

[*194*] (1) Ibid., p. 106. "There is nothing . . . to play with."
(2) Richards, "Complementary Complementarities," op. cit., p. 36. "that's not how . . . well be none."
(3) Eliot, "Four Quartets," op. cit., p. 129. "Not the intense . . . cannot be deciphered."

[*196*] Richards, "Silences," *The Screens and other Poems,* p. 55. "But listen! When . . . listens: listen again."

NOTES: III

[*203*] Wallace Stevens, "Adagia," in *Opus Posthumous* (New York: Alfred A. Knopf, 1966), p. 168. "The word must . . . question of identity."

[*204*] (1) Ihab Hassan, *The Literature of Silence* (New York: Alfred A. Knopf, 1967), p. 207. "objects are no . . . are their habit."
(2) Ludwig Wittgenstein, *Tractatus Logico-Philosophicus*, trans. D. F. Pears and B. F. McGuiness (New York: The Humanities Press, 1960), p. 115, para 5. 6. "The limits of my language mean the limits of my world."
(3) T. E. Hulme, *Speculations* (New York: Harcourt, Brace & Company, 1924), p. 231. "no longer any refuge in the infinities of grandeur."

[*205*] Wallace Stevens, "Description Without Place," in *The Collected Poems of Wallace Stevens* (New York: Alfred A. Knopf, 1967), p. 339. "observing is completing . . . it in the mind."

[*206*] Hulme, op. cit., p. 223. "The same old . . . good as another."

[*207*] (1) Stevens, "An Ordinary Evening in New Haven," op. cit., p. 474. "words of the . . . of the world."
(2) Ibid., "Things of August," p. 490. "The speech of . . . in what it says."

[*208*] Simone Weil, *Gravity and Grace* (London: Routledge and Paul, 1963), trans. Emma Crawford, p. 542. "A closed door . . . the way through."

[*209*] T. E. Hulme, *Further Speculations* (Lincoln: University of Nebraska Press, 1962), p. 82. "Transfer physical to language."

[*210*] (1) Stevens, "Esthetique Du Mal," op. cit., p. 313. "He disposes the world in categories."

(2) Samuel Beckett, *The Unnamable*, in *Three Novels by Samuel Beckett* (New York: Grove Press, 1955), p. 326. "There's no getting . . . keep in mind."

[*211*] Beckett, *Molloy*, op. cit., p. 31. "The icy words . . . the words know."

[*212*] David Pears, *Ludwig Wittgenstein* (New York: The Viking Press, 1962), p. 179. "Meaning and necessity . . . which embody them."

[*213*] Alain Robbe-Grillet, *For a New Novel*, trans. Richard Howard (New York: Grove Press, 1965), p. 19. "neither significant nor . . . splendid construction collapses."

[*214*] (1) Victor Gioscia, "Frequency and Form," in *Radical Software*, No. 2, 1970, p. 7. "Universe is not . . . at varying distances." "Universe is not . . . facade of omniscience."

(2) Wittgenstein, *Tractatus*, p. 149, para. 6.44. "not how things . . . that it exists."

[*217*] Advertisement for "Friends of the Earth," reprinted in *The Whole Earth Catalog Supplement*. "everyone talks about . . . this way fast."

[*218*] Hugo von Hofmannsthal, *Selected Prose*, trans. Mary Hottinger and Tania & James Stern (New York: Pantheon Books, 1952), p. 182. "where is this . . . Here! Or nowhere."

[*219*] Norman O. Brown, "Daphne or Metamorphosis," in *Myths, Dreams, and Religions*, ed. Joseph Campbell (New York: E. P. Dutton & Co., 1970), p. 108. "the whole story . . . our very eyes."

[*220*] (1) Robbe-Grillet, op. cit., p. 33. "To tell a story has become strictly impossible."

(2) Beckett, *Molloy*, op. cit., p. 32. "Saying is inventing . . . You invent nothing."

(3) Brown, op. cit., p. 93. "Saying makes it so."

[*222*] Beckett, *The Unnamable*, op. cit., p. 386. "I'm in words . . . all these strangers."

[*223*] Stevens, "Two Prefaces," in *Opus Posthumous*, p. 270. "The god that . . . the question itself."

[*224*] Beckett, *The Unnamable*, op. cit., p. 390. "The thing said . . . a common source."

[*225*] Shakespeare. "A world full . . . signifying nothing."

[*226*] E. E. Cummings, *I* (Cambridge: Harvard University Press, 1969), p. 69. in any number of . . . "past," "present," or "future."

[*227*] (1) Hulme, *Speculations*, p. 221. "it is impossible . . . the symbolic language."

(2) Stevens, "Final Soliloquy of the Interior Paramour," in *Collected Poems*, p. 524. "Here, now, we . . . in the mind."

[*228*] Stevens, "As You Leave the Room," in *Opus Posthumous*, p. 117. "nothing has been . . . changed at all."

[*230*] (1) Paul Valery, *The Outlook For Intelligence* (New York: Harper & Row, 1962), p. 157. "All the notions . . . calling the tune."

(2) Ibid., p. 162. "the real is . . . carry much weight."

[*231*] Robbe-Grillet, op. cit., p. 148. "description comes to . . . creation and destruction."

[*233*] Valery, op. cit., p. 68. "once speculation was . . . no longer conceivable."

[*234*] Ibid., p. 69. "simply that our . . . is positively transcendent."

[*235*] Stevens, "Connoisseur of Chaos," in *Collected Poems*, p. 215. "The squirming facts exceed the squamous mind."

[*238*] Hassan, op. cit., p. 127. "the facts of . . . doubt on both."

[*241*] Ezra Pound, "Ortus," in *Personae* (New York: New Directions, 1926), p. 84. "I beseech you . . . but a being."

[*243*] (1) Stevens, "The Rock," op. cit., p. 525. "The lives lived . . . to be believed."

(2) Ibid., "Chocorua To Its Neighbor," p. 298. "He was not . . . existing everywhere."

[*245*] Robbe-Grillet, op. cit., p. 147. "once claimed to . . . to disappear altogether."

[*247*] Stevens, "United Dames of America," op. cit., p. 206. "The mass is . . . man of the mass."

[*250*] Ibid., "The Rock," p. 525. "it is an illusion that we were ever alive."

[*251*] Ludwig Wittgenstein, *Philosophical Investigations*, trans. G. E. M. Anscombe (New York: The Macmillan Company, 1958), p. 48, para. 115. "A picture held . . . to us inexorably."

[*253*] Robbe-Grillet, op. cit., p. 23. "we had thought . . . all its life."

[*254*] Stevens, "St. Armorer's Church from the Outside," op. cit., p. 529. "No sign of . . . as its symbol."

[*255*] (1) Weil, op. cit., p. 28. "decreation: to make . . . to the uncreated."

(2) Wallace Stevens, *The Necessary Angel* (New York: Random House, Inc., 1951), p. 175. "Modern reality is . . . our own powers."

[*256*] Weil, op. cit., p. 29. "we participate in . . . by decreating ourselves."

[*257*] Stevens, "Adagia," in *Opus Posthumous*, p. 169. "Life is the elimination of what is dead."

[*258*] (1) Beckett, *The Unnamable*, op. cit., pp. 394–95. "There was never . . . me of me."

(2) Valery, op. cit., p. 40. "When I dream . . . I not . . . Nature?"

[*260*] Brown, op. cit., p. 100. "a fall into . . . natural object: 'projected.'" "the death of . . . birth of poetry."

[*261*] (1) Ibid., p. 107 (quoting Blake). "each herb and . . . men seen afar.

(2) Von Hofmannsthal, op. cit., p. 349. "man perceives in . . . needs the world."

[*262*] Pears, op. cit., p. 4. "need any justification . . . center, man himself."

[*264*] Beckett, op. cit., p. 404. "the fault of . . . comes from that."

[*265*] Ibid., pp. 334–35. "it's a lot . . . of such expressions."

[*266*] Hassan, op. cit., p. 119. "Combat all rationalist . . . a metaphysical universe."

[*268*] Paul Valery, *Masters and Friends: The Collected Works of Paul Valery, Vol. 9*, ed. Jackson Matthews, trans. Martin Turnell (Princeton: Princeton University Press, 1968), p. 69. "made a personal . . . tipped the balance."

[*269*] (1) Henry Miller, *The Wisdom of the Heart* (New York: New Directions, 1941), p. 169. "own validity . . . and unthinkable order."

(2) Weil, op. cit., p. 34. "Uproot yourself . . . every earthly country."

[*272*] Paul Valery, *History and Politics: The Collected Works of Paul Valery, Vol. 10*, ed. Jackson Matthews, trans. Denise Folliot and Jackson Matthews (New York: Pantheon Books, 1962), p. 222. "How can anyone . . . curiosities, a masquerade."

[*273*] Beckett, op. cit., p. 388. "It has not . . . midst of silence."

[*275*] (1) Valery, *Outlook For Intelligence*, p. 136. "our kind of . . . in their solution."

(2) Robbe-Grillet, op. cit., p. 14. "to illustrate a . . . such to themselves."

[*277*] Stevens, "The Creations Of Sound," in *Collected Poems*, pp. 310–11. "there are words . . . an artificial man."

[*278*] (1) Ibid., "Dutch Graves In Bucks County," p. 292. "Freedom is like . . . an incessant butcher."

(2) Ibid., "Chaos In Motion And Not In Motion," p. 358. "He has lost the whole in which he was contained."

[279] Robbe-Grillet, op. cit., p. 68. "Drowned in the . . . impressions and desires."

[281] (1) Ibid., p. 51. "to recover *everything* . . . as a whole."
(2) Ibid., p. 58. "A common nature . . . to everything: man."

[282] (1) Hulme, *Speculations*, p. 166. "Man is an . . . is absolutely constant."
(2) Robbe-Grillet, op. cit., p. 75. "Man is a sick animal." (quoting Unamano). "Imprison him in the disease."

[283] Stevens, "Less And Less Human, O Savage Spirit," op. cit., p. 328. "the human that . . . incommunicable mass."

[284] Beckett, *Molloy*, op. cit., p. 110. "From their places . . . and as bound."

[285] Stevens, "The Common Life," op. cit., p. 221. "The men have no shadows." "A man is a result, a demonstration."

[286] Hassan, op. cit., p. 207. "the role of . . . are their habit."

[288] Valery, op. cit., p. 42. "I can find . . . itself are myths."

[289] (1) Brown, op. cit., p. 109. "Private authorship or . . . all one book."
. . . with their language."
(2) Beckett, *The Unnamable*, op. cit., p. 325. "it's of me

[290] Beckett, Ibid., pp. 299–300. "I must not try to think, simply utter." "I shall have . . . encumbered this place."